Walks in
HISTORIC
KENT

BEA COWAN

COUNTRYSIDE BOOKS

NEWBURY, BERKSHIRE

COUNTRYSIDE BOOKS
3 Catherine Road
Newbury, Berkshire

To view our complete range of books,
please visit us at
www.countrysidebooks.co.uk

ISBN 1 85306 613 3

Designed by Graham Whiteman
Photographs by the author
Maps by Philippa Gillatt

Produced through MRM Associates Ltd., Reading
Printed by J. W. Arrowsmith Ltd., Bristol
Typeset by Techniset Typesetters, Newton-le-Willows

Contents

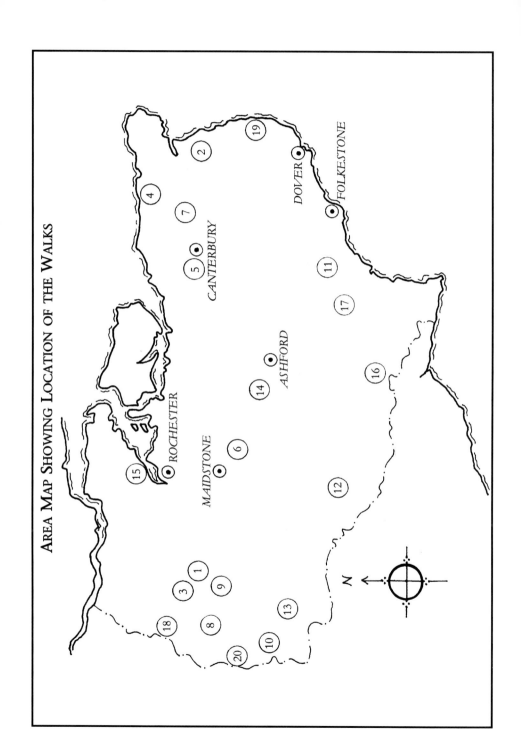

Area Map Showing Location of the Walks

PUBLISHER'S NOTE

We hope that you obtain considerable enjoyment from this book; great care has been taken in its preparation. Although at the time of publication all routes followed public rights of way or permitted paths, diversion orders can be made and permissions withdrawn.

We cannot of course be held responsible for such diversion orders and any inaccuracies in the text which result from these or any other changes to the routes nor any damage which might result from walkers trespassing on private property. We are anxious though that all details covering the walks are kept up to date and would therefore welcome information from readers which would be relevant to future editions.

Introduction

K ent has a varied and rich history and some of the most beautiful walking country in England. By its proximity to Europe the area has always been at the forefront of exchange. The earliest settlers walked here from Europe. Later, after the North Sea had forced its way through the chalk to form the English Channel, they came by sea. Celts, Romans and Saxons all set foot in Kent. When, at the end of the 6th century AD St Augustine landed at Ebbsfleet and reintroduced Christianity to the country, it was in Kent that the first major changes took place and from Kent that monastic and parish models spread out. After the Norman invasion of 1066, kings and queens passed through Kent at regular intervals, while the inns of Kent saw many a traveller carry news to or from distant places. Trade made its mark, sharpening Kent's contact with Europe through the woollen industry or adding zest in the dangerous days of smuggling.

This collection of 20 walks explores some of the loveliest parts of Kent and its greatest houses such as Penshurst Place, Ightham Mote, Hever, Chartwell and Leeds Castle. There are views to be enjoyed across the High Weald, or out over the Channel waters; orchard, riverside and downland paths to be walked – and all the while the main feature of each walk reflects the variety of events which took place within this county. Neolithic farmers, Romans and Saxons appear, a priest, several kings and queens, a poet and a scientist. War sometimes forms a backdrop to events, for, being so close to Europe, defence was long an issue, whether it was the work of the Confederation of the Cinque Ports in the Middle Ages or the labours of the 6th Flotilla in the First World War. There are revolts too, for Kent was a rebellious county. And throughout, I hope, emerge the ordinary men and women of Kent who helped to build the history.

With two exceptions these are country walks. They vary in length between 2 and 7½ miles, but the majority are short, allowing plenty of time to explore the history of the area. All walks are circular, starting at the memorable site or leading the reader to it and back. Grid references are given, both for the starting point and for the site of interest should this be different. At all times on your walk you will find yourself on well-established rights of way. Usually the walk starts from a pub, often itself a place of historic interest. All the pubs recommended welcome walkers and families and you will find that welcome friendly. The pub times of opening may change so there is a telephone number so that you can ring and check. Provided you are a patron/client of the pub you may normally leave your car in the pub car park, but please do ask your host beforehand.

A nearby place of interest is described, often with a related history, so that you may extend your day if you wish. Sketch maps are included for your guidance but you will inevitably find more detail if you use the relevant Ordnance Survey map. The smaller scale OS Landranger (1:50,000) covers a wider area but the new OS Explorer (1:25,000) has more detail and is the better map for walkers. The latter covers more than the older Pathfinder of the same scale which you may well have from earlier days and it shows the more up-to-date rights of way where these have changed, as indeed some have.

I should like to thank all those who have helped me to prepare this selection of walks. I am indebted to the many people who have researched the history and the subject before me, and to all those who have walked and marked the routes. I would like to thank my cousin, Mary, who accompanied me on several of the routes and, above all, my husband, George. He nobly prepared the sketch maps in their first stages and joined me on a number of the walks and shared the interest of them all.

Bea Cowan

WALK 1

A NEOLITHIC BURIAL – THE COLDRUM STONES AT TROTTISCLIFFE

Length: 5 miles

The Coldrum Stones

HOW TO GET THERE: Leave the M26 at junction 2A. Turn south to the A25 and turn left after 200 yards. The George is on your left after 1¼ miles as you enter Trottiscliffe.

PARKING: There is parking for patrons beside the George inn.

MAPS: OS Explorer 148; OS Landranger 188 Maidstone & The Weald (GR 640603; Coldrum Stones 654608).

INTRODUCTION

A walk into prehistory on the slopes below the North Downs, not far from the River Medway in North Kent. This exhilarating walk leads you to the top of the scarp face,

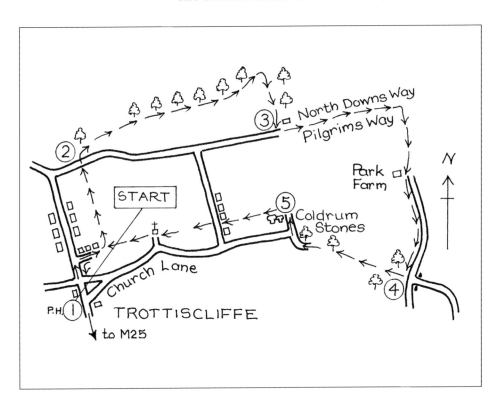

where there is a wide view over the fields the earlier settlers once tilled. It then brings you down to see the Coldrum Stones, their distinctive monument. These are megaliths, huge blocks of sandstone known as sarsen stones, which once surrounded large burial chambers and today are an intriguing and atmospheric reminder of prehistoric times in these parts.

HISTORY

Some time around 2,500 years BC groups of people migrated to Britain from the coast of Northern Europe. Short in stature, with long heads, muscular and good-looking, they came by boat, probably by way of the River Medway. Some found homes on the lower slopes of the North Downs near what is now Trottiscliffe. The land was fertile and the people cultivated it steadily, working with flint carefully shaped into hand-axes or saws. As their remains show, their shin bones became splayed from endlessly squatting while they worked, and rheumatism troubled them when they grew older.

According to their religion, they chose a fine site, looking east towards the Medway, and dug a tomb, 70 feet long and over 50 feet wide. To this site they dragged great blocks of sandstone which they found lying free on the ground in the region. Then they surrounded the tomb with the stones to form a retaining wall. At the east end they made a burial chamber with four large stones at its corners. Inside, they placed their dead – 22 bodies in all. It was a fitting burial place for their people.

THE PLACE

Today you can see what remains of this tomb, where 24 of the huge sarsen stones lie more or less where they were first erected. Others have fallen to the foot of the terrace. You can see the communal burial chamber at the east end where the 22 skeletons, first entombed over 4,000 years ago, were found in 1910.

THE WALK

❶ Turn left as you leave the George and walk up Taylor's Lane. Go ahead at cross-roads. After 100 yards bear right up Green Lane. At the end continue ahead along a bridleway, leaving a fence to your left. Turn left when the fencing ends and walk up the side of a field, leaving gardens to your left. Once past the gardens, walk ahead to the corner of a hedge line, then continue ahead with the hedge on your left. Go through two swing gates and cross a metalled lane.

❷ Go under a barrier into Trosley Country Park. Turn right and walk between wire fences. After 100 yards cross a stile to your left. Bear right and walk up the chalk scarp, following 'Blue Walk no 4.' When you reach fencing, go through a swing gate. Turn right, then almost immediately bear left, uphill, through woodland. Cross a huge tree fallen across the path – there are steps cut into it to help you – and continue to a broad track, the North Downs Way. Turn right and follow the Way to a swing gate beside a green metal barrier. Go through this and walk ahead for 20 yards. Turn sharp right and follow the North Downs Way downhill.

❸ Turn left at a junction beside houses and follow a track used by both the North Downs Way and the Pilgrims' Way. After 3/4 mile, you will reach a stile on your left where a path comes down from the scarp. Here turn right and go downhill between trees. Cross a stile and take a clear path down a broad field. Go ahead onto the road beside a farm. Continue along the road, Park Farm Road, for 500 yards. When you reach April Cottage, just before Chapel Street on your left, cross a stile on your right.

❹ Walk ahead through woodland, going downhill to a broad wooden bridge. Cross the bridge, then walk ahead for 25 yards. Bear right over a stile and follow a grassy track to a stile. Cross the stile and continue ahead through woodland. Where the woodland ends cross another stile. Walk up a

> ### HOSTELRY AND THIRSTQUENCHER
>
> The George at Trottiscliffe gives a great welcome with its old beams and log fires. Here you will find 6X, Masterbrew, Whitbread Best, and Caffreys Irish Ale. You can choose meals such as lambs liver and bacon or home-made pies. Fresh fish is a speciality. The George is open from 11.30 am to 3 pm and from 6 pm to 11 pm weekdays. At weekends it is open all day (Sundays from 12 noon). Telephone: 01732 822462.

A converted oast house in Trottiscliffe

field to the far right-hand corner. Cross a stile and follow the track for 50 yards. Turn right and walk up a farm track for 200 yards. Turn left up steps to reach the Coldrum Stones.

5 Return to the path below the steps. Turn left and walk for 10 yards to a wide field entrance. Turn left and walk up the slope to a field. Now continue ahead, leaving the hedge to your left. At the far side you will enter a narrow lane. Go along this to reach first a car park, then a road. Cross the road. Go over a stile and follow the path ahead towards the church of St Peter and St Paul, Trottiscliffe. Go past the church into a farmyard. Pass a barn and enter the field ahead. Cross the field with the fence to your left. At the far side retrace your steps along the first bridleway of your walk and then along Green Lane. Turn left and walk down the road to return to the George inn.

> **OTHER PLACES OF INTEREST**
>
> You can visit two more prehistoric burial chambers, Kit's Coty House and Little Kit's Coty House, which are still standing. You will find them just west of the A229, 2 miles north of Maidstone. (OS 148; GR 744608 and 743604.)

Walk 2

Triumphal Entry – The Roman Fort at Richborough

Length: 4 miles

The remains of the Saxon Shore Fort

HOW TO GET THERE: Take the road running east from the junction of the A257 Canterbury-Sandwich road and the A256 Dover-Ramsgate road. Continue when this narrows until you see the Bell Hotel ahead of you. To reach the Quay turn left, then immediately right, just before the Barbican.

PARKING: There is one car park beside the Quay at Sandwich, to the east of the Barbican; another at the Cattle Market from where you have easy access to Rope Walk.

MAPS: OS Explorer 150; OS Landranger 179 Canterbury & East Kent (GR 333582; Richborough Fort 324602).

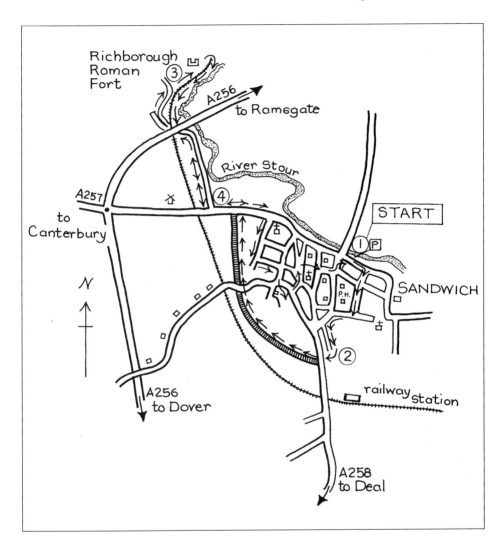

INTRODUCTION

A fascinating walk full of historical interest, which takes you to the site of one of the grandest monuments of Roman Britain. To reach it you set out from Sandwich, starting at The Quay beside the River Stour, to follow part of the old Town Wall before heading towards the Roman fort of Rutupiae at Richborough. Here are the majestic ruins of the Saxon Shore Fort which arose around the 1st century Roman town. You return beside the River Stour, then have the chance to explore more of ancient Sandwich, a Cinque Port from the Middle Ages.

HISTORY

The Roman port of Rutupiae stood at the eastern end of the Wantsum Channel, the waterway which lay between the Isle of Thanet and the mainland of Britain. At the end of the 1st century AD the port was a hive of activity. It was little over 50 years since the Roman troops had, in 43 AD, made a bridgehead here before advancing steadily to take the rest of Britain. Now, while the fighting fleet was stationed at Dover, 15 miles down the coast, here at Rutupiae the chief activity was trade. Wine, oil, olives and fruit arrived in abundance. In return were exported the outstanding oysters for which the nearby Thames estuary had become famous.

This was the entrance to the Roman province of Britannia and to mark the importance of the site, a huge four-way arch, 88 feet high and 48 feet wide, towered over all in the centre of the town. It was cased in white marble specially brought from northern Italy, and bore delicate carvings. No Roman arriving here would have any doubt that Britannia was a flourishing and important place.

THE PLACE

Numerous finds have been excavated at Richborough from that period, balances and weights, including one in the form of a bearded satyr, and many pieces of pottery from the amphorae that carried the perishable goods. Nothing now remains of the Roman archway that offered such a triumphal entry to visitors arriving in Britain by way of Rutupiae but you can see where it stood and the area it covered. Surrounding it are the impressive walls surviving from the later so-called Saxon Shore Fort constructed when the Romans felt their control weaken and feared that marauding Saxons would invade the province. The site belongs to English Heritage (entry fee required) and all is explained if you use their audio-guide and visit the excellent museum beside the fort. There you can see Roman artefacts and find good displays. Open all year round: daily from 1st April to 1st November; Wednesday to Sunday in November; Saturday and Sunday between December and February; Wednesday to Sunday in March. Telephone: 01304 612013.

THE WALK

❶ With your back to the river at the Quay, go through the arch of Fisher Gate and walk up Quay Lane. Pass the Old Custom House on the left-hand corner, cross Upper Strand Street and walk ahead up Fisher Street. You will find the George and Dragon on the right-hand side. When you reach a T-junction, turn right into Church Street, then left into The Chain. Follow The Chain to the right, then turn left into Mill Wall Place. Climb the steps up to Mill Wall.

> **HOSTELRY AND THIRSTQUENCHER**
>
> There are several good hostelries in Sandwich. We recommend the George and Dragon in Fisher Street. You could try a fish dish or one of their pizzas, home-made on their wood-burning stove. Their light ales are changed regularly and will not disappoint. There is a good wine list and the coffee is great. Opening times are from 11 am to 3 pm and from 6 pm to 11 pm every day; from 12 noon on Sunday. Telephone: 01304 613206.

The Barbican, Sandwich

❷ Turn right along part of the Town Wall and walk for 200 yards to New Street. Cross, leaving the Sandwich Arms on the far right-hand corner. Continue along Ropewalk, with the moat below you on your left. Cross Moat Sole and continue along the old wall, now named The Butts. Cross the main road, Ash Road. Turn left, then take the first road to your right, Richborough Road. Walk for 1 mile to the outer entrance to Rutupiae, the old Roman fort at Richborough. Go through the open gateway and walk through the car park to a small gate leading onto the site.

❸ To continue the walk, take the narrow, fenced footpath 50 yards to the right of the small gate and walk along it, leaving the fort to your left. Go down steps. Cross a stile. Turn right immediately. Go over another stile and cross the railway. Turn right immediately and follow a broad, grass path beside the Great Stour. Cross a bridge and a stile, then go ahead. Walk under the A256 and join the Richborough Road. Turn left and continue to the main road.

OTHER PLACES OF INTEREST

Sandwich is a joy to explore. The town developed as an important harbour on a spit of land beside the Wantsum and became a leading town of the Confederation of Cinque Ports during the Middle Ages. These ports were given trading privileges in return for their help in naval defence. The town contains a host of medieval buildings and roads whose layout has changed little since Domesday. Its history is told in the buildings themselves and in the Guildhall Museum – telephone: 01304 613565.

❹ When you reach Ash Road, turn left. The road narrows into Strand Street. When you see St Mary's church on a far right-hand corner, turn right along Church Street. Take the second turning left into Delf Street. Turn right into Cattle Market, then left into New Street. Pass the Guildhall and Museum on your right. Turn left and cross New Street. Walk the short length of No Name Street, then go ahead at the crossroads. Continue along Market Street. Turn right and follow the path to the left of St Peter's church. Cross St Peter's Street. Turn left. Almost immediately, turn right and walk along Seven Post Alley. Turn left along High Street. Leave the end of Upper Strand Street to your right. Pass the Bell Hotel on your right and the Crispin Inn on your left. Turn right before the Barbican to reach the car park beside the Quay.

WALK 3

A MOST DESIRABLE RESIDENCE –
LULLINGSTONE ROMAN VILLA

Length: 2 miles

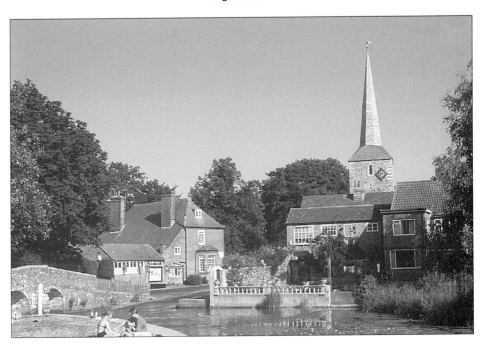

HOW TO GET THERE: Eynsford lies on the A225 Dartford to Sevenoaks road. If taking the road south from the A20, after 1 mile turn right in Eynsford village, following the sign to Lullingstone Castle. Cross the bridge beside the ford. The Plough is on your right, just beyond the river.

PARKING: You will find a good car park beside the Plough. There is also a car park beside the Roman villa, if you want to start from there but please note that this is locked when the villa closes.

MAPS: OS Explorer 162; OS Landranger 177 East London (GR 539656; Lullingstone Roman Villa 530652).

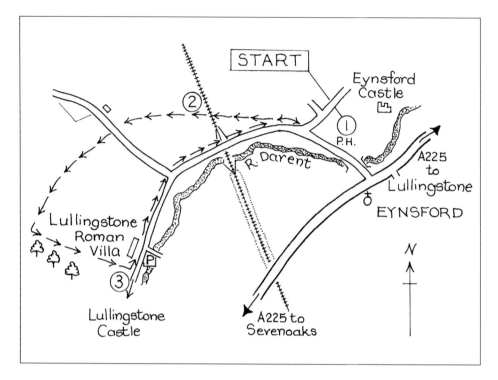

Introduction

A walk in the lovely Darent valley that takes you to one of the best preserved Roman villas in the whole of England. You set out from the village of Eynsford, with its pack-horse bridge and ford, walking uphill for a stretch for a fine view over the valley, before returning to the riverside. There you will be able to see for yourself something of the luxurious life-style of a well-to-do Roman Briton.

History

The Darent valley had always been a popular place to live. From the earliest times men had made homes for themselves, first on the downland slopes above, later in the valley bottom itself, beside the clear waters of the chalk stream. In Roman times the area was stable and prosperous and you would have found at least six villas beside the river between Otford and Dartford, nearly a villa every mile. And in around 350 AD a new owner came to live at the bend in the river. At Lullingstone he had found the perfect place. After a period of recession, prosperity had at last returned to the country and he had great designs for his property. The site was ideal – fertile land, a clear stream to power a corn mill, woodlands to provide unlimited supplies of timber for building and fuel. The family would enjoy a pleasant view. He could reach Londinium with ease.

The villa was old and sadly run down. Rebuilding began immediately. Outside, the new owner improved the granary beside the river, to make sure of a plentiful supply of grain throughout the year. Inside, he ensured that the bath house which lay to the south of the villa was in perfect order. With its hot room, cold room and furnace for heating the water, that was an essential for good living. But with neighbours to north and south in the valley, and entertaining to be done, it was the building of the large, apsed dining room and the audience chamber that pleased him most. He summoned craftsmen and had them lay the finest mosaic floors money could buy. With marble from abroad and local stone they showed well-known stories from Greek mythology and even had a quotation from the Roman poet, Virgil, to impress.

THE PLACE

The Roman villa, first built around 75 AD, underwent many alterations before it was destroyed by fire early in the 5th century. Excavations, started in 1949, revealed not only the bath house and the once-luxurious mosaics, but the ingenious underfloor system which heated the place. Most remarkable of all, however, are the signs of Christian worship in the villa for, later in the 4th century, a chapel was installed over the cellar and the distinctive Chi-rho monogram painted on its south wall. You can see the bath house and mosaics when you visit the site. You can also see a copy of the Chi-rho monogram (the remains are kept in the British Museum, in London, within a full reconstruction of the chapel). Lullingstone Roman Villa is owned by English Heritage who explain the background and the history with a good audio-guide, and have further written guides to interpret. Open daily 1st April to 1st November, 10 am to 6 pm; 2nd November to 31st March, 10 am to 4 pm. Telephone: 01322 863467.

THE WALK

❶ Turn right as you leave the car park of the Plough and walk up the road, appropriately named Riverside. You see the River Darent flowing on your left. Pass the end of Sparepenny Lane on your right, and then walk past Darenth Cottage. Just past Hulberry Farm, turn right and go through a narrow space to the left of a gate. Follow the walk sign diagonally up the field. Cross a stile leading onto a foot crossing over the railway. Listen carefully for the hooter of any train approaching, and cross the railway carefully when you are sure none is coming.

❷ Cross a stile into a field. Soon you have a fine view over the Darent valley at Eynsford. Continue uphill towards a line of trees. Cross a stile, cross a lane, then cross another stile into a field. Follow the path until you reach a stile

HOSTELRY AND THIRSTQUENCHER

Eynsford has several inns and pubs along its main street, especially to the south of the turning to Lullingstone. Most convenient for your walk is the Plough, to the west of the main road and beside an attractive stretch of the River Darent. Here you will find Boddington Draught, Wadworth 6X and Pedigree among other ales. Menus are based on British fare and you will find good helpings of traditional meals. Open all day, every day. Telephone: 01322 862281.

leading onto a tree-lined lane. Cross the stile, then turn left and walk downhill. Go on past a stile in a wooded area and continue until you reach steps leading onto a narrow road.

❸ Turn left. Here you find the Roman villa on your left. Its car park lies to your right. To return to Eynsford village, continue along the small road, Lullingstone Lane. Go under the railway viaduct, then follow the road round when you reach the beginning of Eynsford village and return to the Plough.

OTHER PLACES OF INTEREST

Lullingstone Castle, beside the River Darent, is said to have been a favourite haunt of Henry VIII and Anne Boleyn. Reached from the A225, just south of Eynsford, it is open between April and October on Saturday, Sunday and Bank Holidays between 2 pm and 6 pm. Telephone: 01322 862114. The attractive church of St Botolph at Lullingstone has bricks and tiles removed in medieval times from the Roman villa incorporated in its brickwork. Lullingstone Park Visitor Centre, 1/2 mile south of Eynsford, has an interesting display of local history and explanations of wild life, as well as a good café. Telephone: 01322 865995.

WALK 4

FROM ROMAN FORT TO CHRISTIAN MINSTER – BASSA'S ABBEY AT RECULVER

Length: 3¹/₂ miles

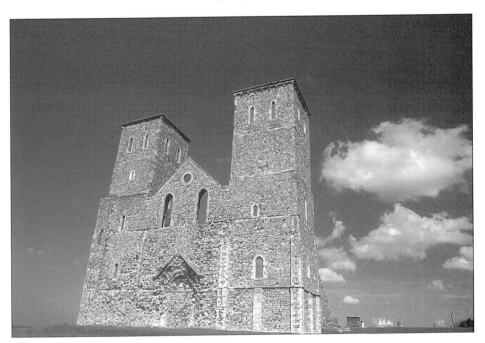

St Mary's Tower

HOW TO GET THERE: Reculver lies to the east of Herne Bay, and can be reached through Hillborough off the A299.

PARKING: There is a good car park beside the road as you approach Reculver.

MAPS: OS Explorer 150; OS Landranger 179 Canterbury & East Kent (GR 228693).

INTRODUCTION
This marvellous walk takes you back through more than 1,500 years of history. You walk from Reculver Roman Fort by fields where boundaries have not changed since

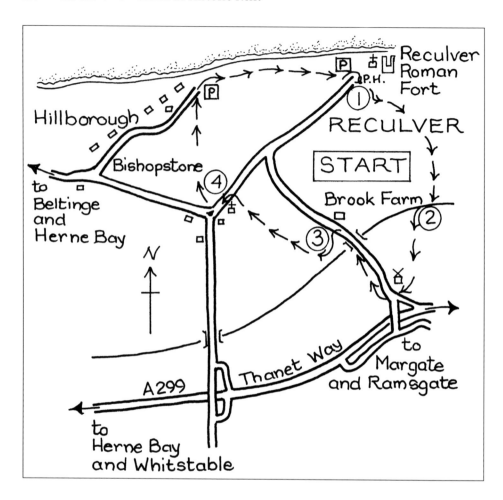

Saxon times, and return downhill with an amazing view of coastline, sea, and, in season, migrating birds in flight. But the highlight of the walk is what was one of the most important early churches in Kent, if not the country – Bassa's Abbey of St Mary, founded on the site of the old fort in the 7th century. Its solitary twin towers added in the 13th century still remain.

History

It is not only the passing of time that has obscured events which took place at Reculver in early Saxon days. Steady erosion by the sea, as it wore away the cliff to the north side of the old Saxon Shore Fort that replaced the first Roman fort, and the haphazard removal of parts of the buildings by later people have also taken their toll. Thankfully we have written records to provide witness to a moment in AD 669 when King Egbert gave the old site of Reculver to a priest named Bassa, with precise instructions to found a monastery on the site.

It was less than a century since Egbert's predecessor, Ethelbert, and his wife, Queen Bertha, had welcomed St Augustine after he arrived at Ebbsfleet at the eastern end of the Wantsum Channel. With the building in Canterbury, first of St Augustine's monastery, then of Christ Church Cathedral itself, Ethelbert had ensured that Christianity was reintroduced into Britain after a lapse of several centuries. Now at Reculver, using many of the bricks and tiles first used by the Romans when they had a fort here, Bassa built a monastery which was to dominate the region for several centuries. All but destroyed during the terrible period in the late 9th century when Vikings marauded along the coast, it just managed to survive and eventually passed into the hands of Christ Church, Canterbury, 300 years after Bassa first carried out King Egbert's instructions.

THE PLACE

You can see the remains of Bassa's church, aligned due east, within the boundaries of the Roman fort. Soon to become St Mary's Abbey, it was built with rubble stone and flint, with bands of Roman tile from the earlier fort. The towers were added in the 13th century. Romans first built the fort in the 1st century, along with Rutupiae (see Walk 2) to defend the Wantsum Channel, then they reinforced it as a Saxon Shore Fort in the 3rd century. In 1805 local people removed most of the church to Hillborough, partly because they feared it would be lost to erosion. The distinctive twin towers survived as navigation markers for shipping. The site belongs to English Heritage and is open at all times (no entry charge). A first-rate Information Centre beside the car park has displays and some exhibits which explain much more of this fascinating place.

THE WALK

❶ From the King Ethelbert turn left along the road, and walk past a children's playground to your left. Turn left at a phone box and walk along a concrete track. Continue ahead, as this becomes a gravelly farm track. Turn right just before a gateway. Follow a path along a field headland, with a dyke to your right. Continue first with a small dyke to your right, then a hedge. Cross a stock-proof bridge and continue to a stile with a steep bank of trees ahead of you. Cross, then turn right and walk along a concrete track for 25 yards.

❷ Turn left and walk under the railway. Walk up a concrete farm track, leaving kennels on your left. When you reach Chislett Mill turn right. On this

> **HOSTELRY AND THIRSTQUENCHER**
>
> The King Ethelbert, which was built on the site of the old vicarage, extends a fine welcome. The choice of dishes offered is wide, ranging from Barnsley-style lamb chops to Chinese dishes. It is a free house and you will find familiars such as Whitbread's Best Bitter and Flowers Original as well as East Kent Brewery's Best Bitter and the Swale Brewery Company's Kentish Pride. Open all day every day. Food is served from 12 noon to 3 pm and 6.30 pm to 9 pm. Telephone: 01227 374368.

The ruins of St Mary's church

stretch, in particular, you will see on your left some of the old Saxon field boundaries. After ½ mile you will pass an Elizabethan gateway on your left. Pass the entrance to Brook Farm on your right, and a large metal barn on your left.

> **OTHER PLACES OF INTEREST**
>
> Remains of a cross, the Reculver Cross, which stood in Bassa's church, and two columns from the original church, are kept in the crypt of Canterbury Cathedral. St Augustine's Abbey, Canterbury, has traces of a ground plan very similar to St Mary's.

❸ Turn left and follow the footpath sign towards a marker post set above steps in the left-hand hedge line. Here turn your back to the steps and bear left, heading up the field towards the right-hand side of the church of St Mary the Virgin. (The church has no true spire.) Leave a field bridge to your left. Cross a farm track then make for a marker post 150 yards above the field bridge. Cross a dyke and continue on the same line to a marker post. Walk into the church car park.

❹ Turn right to reach the road, then turn left. Take a right-hand fork and bear right into Reculver Road. Almost immediately turn right into the corner of a field. Follow the sign on a telegraph pole. Bear left and walk across the field for 200 yards, to a point just to the right of a concrete path and buildings. Turn right and walk across the field, aiming for the end of a line of houses on the far side. Cross a land bridge exactly in line with the last house ahead and continue. Cross a stile leading onto the road. Turn right and continue to the end of the road. Enter the Reculver Country Park and follow a well-trodden path downhill for 1 mile to return. You are drawn on by the distinctive Reculver towers.

WALK 5

A TURBULENT PRIEST? THE MURDER OF
THOMAS À BECKET AT CANTERBURY

Length: 2¹/₂ miles

St Augustine's Abbey, with Christ Church Cathedral beyond

HOW TO GET THERE: Take the A28 from Ashford, the A2050 from the A2 (both from north and south), the A290 from Whitstable, the A28 from Ramsgate or the A257 from Sandwich. St Augustine's Abbey, at the start of the walk, lies to the east of the city centre, on the A257.

PARKING: Recommended are the long stay parks at the junction of Longport and Lower Chantry Lane, beside St Augustine's Abbey (A257) and on the north-east side of the city, in Northgate, south-east of the A28. Car parks around the city are all clearly signed.

MAPS: OS Explorer 150; OS Landranger 179 Canterbury & East Kent (GR 155577).

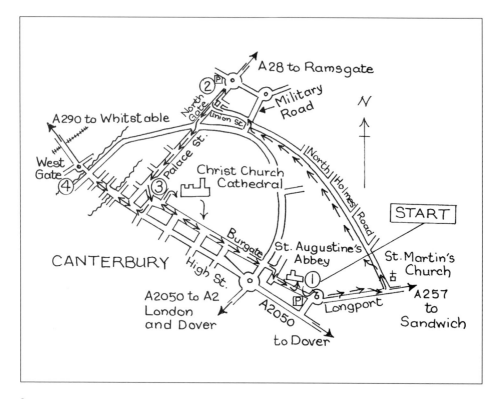

INTRODUCTION

A walk through the ancient streets of Canterbury to the place, in the Cathedral Church of Christ, where Archbishop Thomas à Becket was murdered in 1170. Here are the splendid Trinity chapel built with money given by pilgrims and the amazing stained glass windows portraying the miracles the saint was said to have performed after his death. The route begins at St Augustine's Abbey, the first monastery to be founded in England. Later you walk along St Peter's Street and savour some more of this wonderful city's historical sites.

HISTORY

'Will no one rid me of this turbulent priest?' cried Henry II as he fumed against his Archbishop, Thomas à Becket. Four knights heard Henry's outburst of frustration and at twilight on 29th December 1170 they burst, fully armed, into the Cathedral Church of Christ in Canterbury. They made their way to the chapel where the Archbishop was praying at vespers. There was a brief argument, then one of them drew his sword and stabbed the Archbishop as he knelt.

Becket's death, thought by the knights to be the wish of their king, Henry II, brought profound distress. At one time Becket had served the King faithfully as statesman and diplomat, but since he had become archbishop in 1164, Becket had stood firm against the King's moves to curb the power of the church. He saw what Henry considered essential reforms as state interference in church affairs. But the murder shocked the King deeply. The people of England and, indeed all Christendom, were appalled. Soon tales of miraculous cures spread and Becket was declared a martyr. He was canonised in 1173, while in 1174 Henry made penance in the Cathedral. In 1220 a new chapel was built to the east of the high altar and the shrine established there. The site became the most popular shrine in Europe for pilgrimage and for the next 300 years pilgrims flocked to visit it.

The Place

Christ Church Cathedral is a memorable place. It was first built by St Augustine in AD 602, rebuilt by the Norman, Lanfranc, in 1070, then largely rebuilt again with money brought by the thousands of pilgrims who visited the shrine of St Thomas à Becket. From the outside you see the tower, Bell Harry. Inside, you see the great choir, some of which survives from before a fire of 1174. Canterbury Cathedral is open to visitors from 9 am until 5.30 pm from Monday to Friday; from 9 am until 2 pm on Saturday; from 12.30 pm until 2.30 pm and from 4.30 pm until 5.30 pm on Sunday.

The Walk

Before you begin the walk, you may like to visit St Augustine's Abbey, the centre of St Augustine's movement. You can see the remains of the earliest part of the abbey and there is a superb exhibition as you enter. It is open every day from 10 am to 6 pm April to September, 10 am until 5 pm in October and 10 am until 4 pm from November until March. It is owned by English Heritage so there is an entry fee, well worthwhile.

❶ Turn left as you leave St Augustine's Abbey. Walk past the roundabout and along Longport (the A257). Leave HM Prison to your left. Take the first turning left along North Holmes Road. You will see St Martin's church ahead of you. Continue for 1/2 mile. Go between the black-painted iron posts and cross Old Ruttington Lane to join the main road, Military Road. Turn right, and cross this busy road at the crossing. Go slightly left and then ahead into Union Street.

❷ Turn second left along Northgate. At crossroads, cross, then go ahead into The Borough. Follow the road into Palace Street and continue until you reach a junction of four roads. Bear left into Sun Street. Very soon you find yourself in the square outside Christ Church Cathedral.

❸ Turn left and go through Christ Church Gate and into the cathedral precinct. Go ahead to enter the cathedral. When you leave the cathedral by its main doorway, turn left, then right, to follow

> **HOSTELRY AND THIRSTQUENCHER**
>
> The Weavers Restaurant in St Peter's Street (telephone: 01227 464660) is to be recommended but is just one of many pleasant and friendly hostelries throughout the city. Every taste is provided for and it would not be possible to list all the inns, cafes or restaurants.

Christ Enthroned, Christ Church Gate

the signed exit. You will now find yourself in Burgate. Here turn right and walk to Christ Church Gate, then turn left into Mercery Lane. Turn right along St Peter's Street and continue along this pedestrian area to the traffic junction. St Peter's Place runs to your left, Pound Lane to your right. You will see the West Gate ahead.

❹ Retrace your steps along St Peter's Street. Pass The Chaucer Centre on your left at nos 22–23. Pass The Weavers Restaurant, also on your left, then the Eastbridge Hospital on your right. Continue to Mercery Lane. Here turn left. When you see Christ Church Gate ahead, turn right. Walk along Burgate and continue to the main road, Lower Bridge Street. Cross the road by the pedestrian crossing and go ahead between bollards into Church Street. Turn right, then left into Longport. St Augustine's Abbey is on your left, the car park on your right.

> **OTHER PLACES OF INTEREST**
>
> St Martin's church, where Queen Bertha worshipped even before St Augustine arrived in England, is open from 9 am until 5 pm. Among many other places is Canterbury Castle, with the ruins of the Norman keep and information panels, open from 8 am until dusk. Telephone: Canterbury Tourist Information Centre on 01227 766567.

WALK 6

A CHILD BRIDE AND A QUEEN'S GIFT – LEEDS CASTLE

Length: 2¹/₂ miles

Leeds Castle and moat

HOW TO GET THERE: Leeds village is situated on the B2163, south-east of Maidstone and between the A20 and A274 roads.

PARKING: You will find a useful car park to the south of the church. Patrons may park beside the George.

MAPS: OS Explorer 137 or 148; OS Landranger 188 Maidstone and the Weald (GR 824532; Leeds Castle 836534).

INTRODUCTION

An unforgettable walk that introduces you to Leeds Castle and the Queen who first made it a royal castle, the exceptional Eleanor of Castile, wife of Edward I. You start

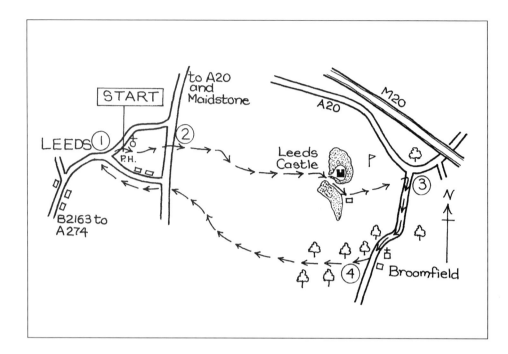

from the village of Leeds where a church has stood since Saxon times, walk through parkland above the castle, then come to the loveliest castle in Kent, bought by Eleanor 800 years ago. The return route is through the quiet village of Broomfield and along high ground above the castle.

HISTORY

In 1254 Eleanor, a Spanish princess and only eight years old, was brought from Castile, to be married to the fifteen-year-old Edward, son of the Plantagenet Henry III. The marriage was propitious in almost every way. Edward, who succeeded his father as king in 1272, was devoted to his wife, while Eleanor came to be a wise and moderating influence on him. She was noble, stately and also practical. In 1278 she borrowed money and bought Leeds Castle as a gift for her husband. In 1290, after 36 years of marriage, she was taken ill at Harbey in Nottinghamshire while Edward was hunting, and later died in his arms. Grief-stricken, Edward built a cross at each of the places her coffin rested on its way to London. The last stop is still known as Charing Cross, from 'chère reine' (dear queen). Then Edward had her body laid to rest in Westminster Abbey. In the chapel at Leeds Castle he established a chantry, and four monks and a clerk were appointed to celebrate a daily mass for Eleanor's soul.

THE PLACE

Leeds Castle stands surrounded by its great moat formed from the River Len which flows through the grounds. It was first built as a motte-and-bailey castle in the 12th century and over the centuries acquired the many fine apartments you can see today – as well as the chapel and chantry there are a gatehouse and a fine hall, as well as a gloriette and Maiden's Tower. The guide book explains it all. Leeds Castle is open every day from 10 am to 5 pm between March and October, 10 am to 3 pm between November and February; closed 26th June, 3rd July and 25th December. Please note that, to explore the grounds and castle, you must enter officially and buy a ticket. Otherwise when walking you must keep to the footpath.

THE WALK

❶ Outside the George turn right and walk beside the B2163. When you reach the Leeds and Broomfield CE Primary School on your left, turn right along the footpath signed for the Len Valley walk. Go through the gate into the churchyard and follow the path to the right of St Nicholas' church. Continue ahead between gravestones. Go through a double wooden gate at the far side of the churchyard and walk ahead. Veer to the left of a house ahead of you, leaving its garden hedge to your right. Go through a wooden gate. Cross the road and go through a gate into the grounds of the Leeds Castle Foundation. Soon you have some beautiful views of the castle in its valley.

❷ Walk ahead leaving the fence to your left. Go through a wooden gate and continue across a playing field to a gate in the fence ahead of you. Bear right. Follow the route marker downhill towards another, set beside a metalled drive. Walk beside the path, continuing over grassland to a wooden gate beside the cattle grid on the metalled drive. Go ahead along the drive, leaving a car park to your right. Walk beside the lake towards the castle gatehouse. Follow the metalled drive as it swings right and continue with the lake to your right and the moat to your left. Where you see signs to the Fairfax Hall ahead, turn left and continue beside the golf course, still on a metalled track. As you approach the entrance Gatehouse, beside the speed limit sign, bear left towards a yellow marker. Continue along a wood-chip path above a green on the golf course. Turn right and follow steps up to the road.

❸ Turn right and follow the road downhill. Turn sharp right, then left, over the River Len. Continue for $1/4$ mile, uphill, to Broomfield village. You will pass St Margaret's church on your left.

❹ Pass the entrance to Church Farmhouse on your left. Almost immedi-

---

HOSTELRY AND THIRSTQUENCHER

The George in Leeds village is a traditional coaching inn, tile hung on the outside and with a good fire inside on winter days. You will find Shepherd Neame beers here such as Strongbow, Masterbrew and Abbey Original Bitter, Spitfire, and Bishop's Finger. Walkers are welcomed and there is a wide range of hot and cold dishes such as bacon and ham raised pie, lemon filled goujons, broccoli or stilton quiche. Opening hours from Monday to Saturday are from 11 am to midnight and on Sunday from 12 noon to 10.30 pm. No food Sunday and Monday. Telephone: 01622 861314.

A view of the castle from woodland

ately, at Pink Cottage, turn right, through its gateway, and walk up a concrete track. Leave a garage to your right and continue up a grassy farm path between hedges. When you come to the end of the tree-line turn right. Now walk above a slope, leaving small trees to your right. Continue along a narrow path. Continue as the track broadens through woodland. Go through a wooden gate and walk along a field headland, leaving a fence to your right. Cross a stile to a field below you. Turn left below the hedge and walk to a gate. Go through a gate, to the right of a cattle grid and walk down a metalled drive. Cross a small road then walk ahead along narrow George Lane. Emerge on to the B2163 just above the George.

> **OTHER PLACES OF INTEREST**
>
> Sutton Valence is an intriguing small town, set above the scarp of the Greensand ridge. Two routes used since at least Roman times came up the scarp and converged just north of the town, one the important route from Rye to Maidstone. The Normans built a stone keep here in the 12th century to watch over them. It is generally open (English Heritage, no entry fee) and gives a marvellous view over the Weald of Kent to the High Weald beyond. (On the A274, 5 miles south of Maidstone; OS map 188, GR 815491.)

WALK 7

THE PEASANTS' REVOLT – THE FAIR MAID OF KENT AND WICKHAMBREAUX

Length: 7¹/₂ miles

Wickhambreaux

HOW TO GET THERE:
Wickhambreaux lies 4¹/₄ miles east of Canterbury and 1 mile north-east of Littlebourne off the A257 from Canterbury to Sandwich.

PARKING: There is some parking for patrons beside the Rose Inn. There is also space around The Green and along some of the road. You may also park at the National Nature Reserve car park north-east of Stodmarsh and start the walk from there.

MAPS: OS Explorer 150; OS Landranger 179 Canterbury & East Kent (GR 221587).

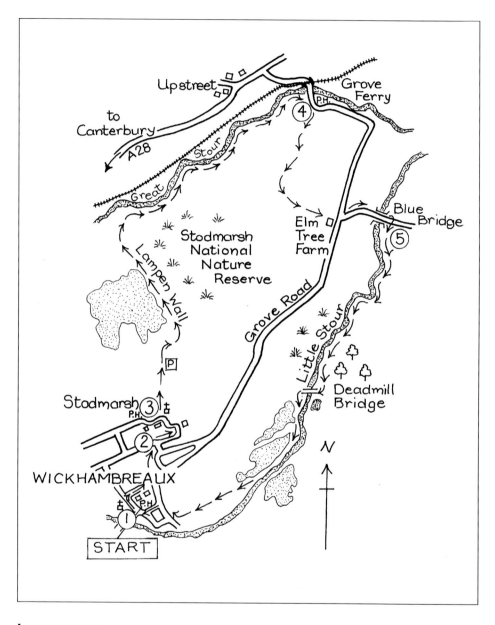

INTRODUCTION

Joan Plantagenet, widow of the dashing and romantic Black Prince, may have reflected often about the peaceful village of Wickhambreaux where her late husband had once courted her. In the terrifying summer of 1381, when peasants rose in rebellion and the whole country erupted in riot and confusion, it might well have seemed a safer place for herself and her son, fourteen-year-old Richard II. This walk takes you from the small village whose manor Joan owned, through orchards and fields to the tiny village of Stodmarsh and its beautiful nature reserve, then beside the Great Stour river to Grove Ferry, once an important river crossing. The return route follows the peaceful Little Stour. This is a longer walk but always on level ground.

HISTORY

Princess Joan Plantagenet was born in 1328, daughter of Edmund, Earl of Kent and granddaughter of Edward I. She grew into a beautiful woman, loved by all, and owned several Kentish manors, including Wickhambreaux. After her first husband's death, she was courted and won by Edward, the Black Prince.

In the summer of 1381 the south of England erupted in riot and confusion. In June, a mixed band of peasants came together in Canterbury to voice their discontent. After the Black Death wages had been set at the levels known before the plague while landowners expected peasants to do more work for the same reward. And in 1371 Parliament had tried to introduce a poll tax. Unrest built up and the peasants in Canterbury, as elsewhere, now demanded redress. Suddenly a leader emerged, Wat Tyler, seemingly from nowhere, though it was known he had been a soldier. With Tyler at their head the peasants marched to London. Joan was also travelling back to London to be with her son, the King, and was disturbed by the sight of so many rebels on the march.

Tyler managed to some extent to control the violence, murder and looting that ensued when they reached London. He withdrew his rabble to the village of Mile End outside the walls of London. There Richard II confronted them. Some people dispersed but others marched on the Tower of London. They stormed the building, killing many and, in her own bedchamber, disturbing no less than Joan, the King's mother herself. Unlike many others in the Tower that day, she was spared. Loved by all, her reputation was such that the most she had to endure was a stubbly kiss before she was hustled away to safety.

THE PLACE

Wickhambreaux, whose manor Joan Plantagenet inherited from her brother, used to be an important stopping place on the way to the ferry over the River Stour at Grove. It is thought that the Black Prince, son of Edward III, wooed Joan in The Old Stone House, to the south-west of the village. Today the village still clusters round its green though most of the medieval houses

---

HOSTELRY AND THIRSTQUENCHER

The 14th-century Rose Inn at Wickhambreaux is open in summer all day every day. To drink you can choose from Young's Special, Green King IPA, and many others. To eat you could try their liver and bacon or one of their home-made meat pies. On Sundays a roast lunch is worth the stay. Telephone: 01227 721763.

The village hostelry

were re-clad in the 18th and 19th centuries.

THE WALK

❶ Turn right outside the Rose Inn. Pass The Rectory and walk to the junction with Grove Road. Turn right. Walk past The List. Cross the road to a stile in a hedge and cross a field to the far right-hand corner. Continue on the same line across the farmyard of Quaives Farm and go through a space to the right-hand side of an iron gate. Walk up the

> **OTHER PLACES OF INTEREST**
>
> The nature reserve at Stodmarsh is a thrilling place for birdwatchers and naturalists. The land was originally drained by the Augustinian monks of Canterbury and used for rearing horses – hence Stod(Stud)marsh. In the 20th century the land subsided because of a nearby colliery and lagoons developed. Now an important wetland habitat, it is managed by English Nature, and you can see many different species of wildfowl and marshland birds.

left-hand side of an orchard. Cross a stile leading onto a metalled farm track. When the main track forks, just in front of a windbreak, continue ahead through an orchard. When you reach a fence, bear left along the headland. Go through a gate into a large field. Go through a gate and bear right. Follow a trodden footpath diagonally across a field, making for a cluster of red roofs in the distance. Step down from the field to a road just before a T-junction.

❷ Turn right and walk for 20 yards. Cross the road, then follow a track diagonally across a field aiming just to the left of a cottage in woods beyond a telegraph pole. Step down to a road and turn left. Follow the road into Stodmarsh. It is well worth going into the tiny church where crusaders used to visit on their way to the Holy Land. Just after the church turn left. Turn right just before the Red Lion and walk up a narrow, metalled lane.

❸ Bear right along a gravelled track towards the Stodmarsh National Nature Reserve car park. As you reach the car park, bear left, and go into the English Nature Reserve. Turn right where you see their sign. Turn left at a junction and follow a clear footpath beside the Great Stour. After 2 miles bear right leaving a garden to your left. Go through a swing gate. Cross the road to the Ferry Inn, or turn immediately right and walk for 100 yards, then turn right.

❹ Follow a gravel path for 300 yards. Where the gravelled path bears left, uphill, you should continue ahead along a grassy path. When you see ahead of you a sign 'Danger – Deep Water', turn left. Follow this path round to the right. At a T-junction turn left. Leave the Reserve through a swing gate, named Point 3. Turn left. Walk along a road for 300 yards. Turn right. Follow the road to the Little Stour. Cross Blue Bridge.

❺ Turn right and follow a footpath, with the river on your right, for 1$\frac{1}{2}$ miles. When you reach the woods turn right down to the river. Cross the river by Deadmill Bridge. Turn left and walk, the river now to your left. Cross a stile and walk along a broad swathe of grass beside the river. Turn right just before a gate and walk along a grassy farm track. Turn left over a stile. Walk to the far right-hand corner of a large field. Cross a stile to the road. Follow the road ahead round to the main road which leads into Wickhambreaux. Turn right and return to the village. You pass The Old Stone House as you enter the village.

WALK 8

ONE DEER PARK TOO MANY – JACK CADE'S
REBELLION NEAR KNOLE

Length: 4¹/₂ miles

Knole House, with its crenellated gateway

HOW TO GET THERE: Godden Green lies 1¹/₂ miles east of Sevenoaks as the crow flies. If you prefer the car, make for the traffic lights on the A25, ³/₄ mile east of the junction with the A225 (known as the Bat and Ball junction), turn south down Seal Hollow Road. Take the second turning left. Turn right after 1 mile to reach Godden Green.

PARKING: There is parking outside the Buck's Head for patrons and limited parking around the Green. You can always park outside Knole itself which is approached from the A225, just south of Sevenoaks town centre, and start the walk from there.

MAPS: OS Explorer 147; OS Landranger 188 Maidstone & the Weald (GR 554547; Knole 539543).

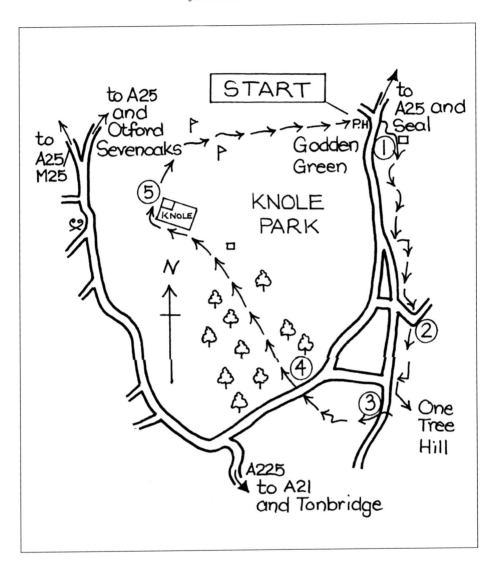

Introduction

In the 15th century Knole was the property of Lord Saye and Sele, Constable of Dover and a harsh landlord. Had he lived to see it, he would have envied the battlemented gatehouse of the house that grew up on the site of his own simpler dwelling. Though built for display alone, those false crenellations would have given him the sense of security he certainly lacked during the last few days of his life, when, in 1450, Jack Cade and his men engaged with the royalist army nearby. On this peaceful walk

Plaque on wall beside Solefields Road commemorating Jack Cade's rebellion.

through woods, then over fields and parkland, you can look towards ground where in the 15th century a group of rebels came to blows with forces of the Crown. You enjoy a wonderful view over the Weald of Kent and pass the famous house of Knole, then return through more parkland to the tiny village of Godden Green. Please note that dogs must be kept on a lead in Knole Park, to protect the deer which roam freely.

HISTORY

The yeomen of Kent complained that the county was mis-governed and justice tainted. More to the point, perhaps, their standard of living was suffering badly since wars in France had prevented exports and the old harbours had been allowed to silt up. And now the Earl of Suffolk, Steward to the weak King Henry VI, had been murdered on board ship as he went into exile, and the men of Kent were blamed for supplying ships to his enemies. Lord Saye and Sele threatened to turn all Kent into a deer park in reprisal. In no time large groups of men from all parts of Kent arrived at Blackheath. Their leader was Jack Cade, who withdrew with them to Solefields near Sevenoaks, less than 1/2 mile from Knole House, home of the detested Lord Saye and Sele. Here Cade hoped to find many more supporters, for the Constable was liked by none. A fierce battle with the royalist army ensued, after which Cade's men advanced on the Tower of London where the Constable had been taken, supposedly for his own safety. The hated man was then taken to the Chepe, now known as Cheapside, to be tried, but the rebels captured and summarily executed him. The rebels dispersed on promise of a general pardon, but Cade was captured soon after while on the run.

THE PLACE

Soon after his father's death, Lord Saye and Sele's son sold his father's property at Knole to Thomas Bourchier, Archbishop of Canterbury, who started the marvellous re-building of the house. To the disappointment of Bourchier's successor, Archbishop Thomas Cranmer, Henry VIII appropriated the property but later Elizabeth I gave it to Thomas Sackville who continued the development. A visit to the mansion built by Bourchier and his successors should not be missed. The house is vast and impressive and contains a rich collection of furniture and paintings. Now owned by the National Trust, it is open from 27th March to 31st October: Wednesday to Saturday 12 noon to 4 pm; Sunday, Good Friday and Bank Holidays 11 am to 5 pm. Telephone: 01892 891001.

THE WALK

❶ Turn right outside the Buck's Head. Walk for 50 yards. Cross the road and follow a driveway towards the Godden Green Clinic. Pass the gateway to the clinic and continue along a gravel track. Walk for 500 yards. When the track swings left, go ahead into woodland. Continue to a stile. Cross, then continue ahead over fields, crossing two stiles. Turn left along a metalled driveway, then continue as this becomes a grass path. Just before you enter the farmyard of Lower Fawke Farm, turn right along a rough metalled track and walk to a road. Turn left. Walk downhill for 250 yards.

❷ Where the road turns sharp left, uphill, turn right along a gravelled track into woodland. Go ahead, uphill, between trees to a T-junction of tracks. Turn right along a broad woodland path to a road. Turn left, then left again into a car park. Cross to the far right-hand corner. Go through a narrow opening in the fence and walk ahead. Take the right-hand fork ahead of you and follow the track for $1/4$ mile. You will see a seat above a slope just to your right. Turn into this open space at One Tree Hill for a quite brilliant view of the Weald of Kent. Turn right and take the track indicated by a Greensand Way sign. Go under a horse barrier and turn left onto the road. Walk downhill for 200 yards.

❸ Bear right up the driveway to Shep-herds Mead. After 20 yards, just before the house gate, turn right. Follow a path for 500 yards. Cross a stile. Turn right. Then bear left up a slope to a stile. Cross a stile, then follow the field edge to the field corner. Turn right. After 120 yards bear left into trees and turn left over a stile. Follow a path through woodland to a road. Cross the road and go through a gateway into Knole Park.

HOSTELRY AND THIRSTQUENCHER

The Buck's Head at Godden Green offers a wide range of excellent meals every day. To drink, it offers Shepherd Neame ales, Strongbow, Guinness, Steinbock lager, Orangeboom, Premium and many others. Please note that there is no food in the evening on Sunday or Monday. Telephone: 01732 761330.

❹ Continue, beside a wire fence to your right. Cross Chestnut Walk and continue along the path ahead. Cross the Broad Walk, and follow a grassy path between bracken. Emerge from the woodland and head for the corner of the property wall of Knole. Continue to the next corner, with the property wall to your right, then turn right. Now you pass the entrance to Knole.

OTHER PLACES OF INTEREST

You can see the place where it is thought the Battle of Solefields may have taken place, at the junction of Solefields Road in Sevenoaks and the A225. A plaque on the wall marks the spot. The market town of Sevenoaks contains many houses of interest, especially in the small streets between Bank Street and the High Street. For the Tourist Information Centre telephone: 01732 450305.

❺ Continue past the 'Teas' sign, unless you are tempted by it, and follow a metalled path through parkland and golf course for ¹/₂ mile. Leave the park through a pedestrian gate set to the right of a large black gate and walk along a sandy track between trees. After 500 yards bear right. Continue to a swing gate and cross a lane. Go through a gate ahead of you and walk past stables. When you reach the road turn right to return to the Buck's Head at Godden Green.

WALK 9

A ROOM FIT FOR A QUEEN – CATHERINE OF ARAGON AT IGHTHAM MOTE

Length: 3¹/₂ miles

Ightham Mote

HOW TO GET THERE: The walk begins at Shipbourne, which lies on the A227 4¹/₂ miles north of Tonbridge and 4 miles south of Borough Green.

PARKING: The Chaser Inn offers some parking and there is usually space beside The Common. Ightham Mote itself has a good car park should you wish to start from there.

MAPS: OS Explorer 147; OS Landranger 188 Maidstone & The Weald (GR 592522; Ightham Mote 585535).

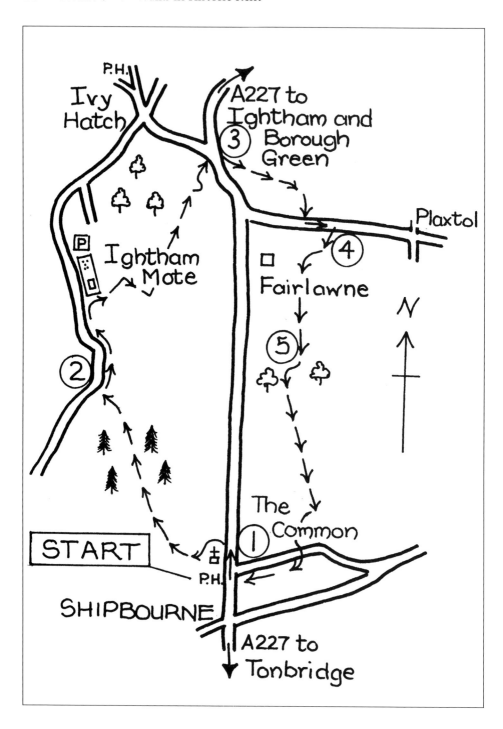

Ightham Mote seen from the small garden

INTRODUCTION

Ightham Mote is one of the most delightful moated manor houses in the country. One part in particular shines out, a room which may well have welcomed Henry VIII and his Queen Catherine, and which still glows with the adornments installed to honour them. To reach this lovely manor house you walk over fields and through woodland on the slopes of the Greensand Ridge, where in season there are carpets of bluebells. There are great views over the Weald of Kent towards Ashdown Forest.

HISTORY

A manor house had stood in the heavily wooded valley of Dinas Dene for nearly 200 years by the time Richard Clement bought it in 1521. He had chosen the place because it was near enough to London for him still to serve at Henry VIII's court yet entertain his own friends in moderate style. Just once he may have brought the King himself, with his Queen, Catherine of Aragon, for in 1525 Clement changed a guest room, which linked the Great Hall with the gatehouse range, into something far more splendid. He installed outstanding barrel-vaulted ceiling timbers decorated with the roses of Lancaster and York, the fleur de lys and the portcullis, the badge of Henry's grandmother which Richard took as his own. For Richard the visit must have proved a success for he was later knighted. For Catherine it was perhaps a last happy event in the years when all else was already working towards her downfall.

THE PLACE

The room where Catherine stayed later became what is now known as the Tudor Chapel. Ightham Mote was first built in the mid-14th century probably by Sir Thomas Cawne. It saw a number of owners, most of whom added to the original great hall and solars, so that now you have the original great hall, with solars and old chapel; a gate house added in the 15th century; the so-called Tudor chapel; a Jacobean drawing room; and Victorian rooms. All are set round a courtyard and surrounded by a moat. The property (National Trust) is open from 27th March to 31st October, daily except Tuesday and Saturday from 11 am to 5.30 pm. Telephone: 01732 811145.

THE WALK

❶ Turn left outside the Chaser Inn. Walk up the gravel path towards St Giles' church. Go through the lych gate, then take the path to the right of the church. Go through the swing gate in the far wall of the churchyard. For once, ignore the official right of way and walk ahead across a field following the signed 'alternative route'. Turn right just past the hedge, then left when you reach a fence ahead of you. Turn right at the next corner. Turn left just beyond a small stream, opposite a stile. Leave to your left a low marker post, then a tall conifer hedge, and follow the path up a field, past a lone oak, to a stile leading into woods. Cross the stile and continue through woods to another stile. Cross this, turn right, then continue down the right-hand side of a field to a stile. Cross and walk to a small road.

❷ Turn right and walk along the road for 200 yards to the entrance to Ightham Mote. Follow the drive past the mansion then continue up the slope to the car park on your left. To enter the property, turn left here and left again after 50 yards to the visitors' entrance. To continue the walk go ahead to hawthorns arching over the path. Turn left almost immediately, following a green arrow, and walk uphill leaving a hedge on your left. At the top of the field go through an open gateway into woodland. Bear right along the right-hand fork and continue through the woods to a gate beside the A227.

> **HOSTELRY AND THIRSTQUENCHER**
>
> The Chaser Inn at Shipbourne remains open all day and welcomes children. Here you will find Courage Directors and Harvey's Sussex Best Beer. A good range of sandwiches is on offer as well as a wide and interesting variety of well-cooked meals. Telephone: 01732 810360. At Ightham Mote there is an excellent Tea House.

> **OTHER PLACES OF INTEREST**
>
> East of Plaxtol lies Old Soar Manor, another National Trust property, open from 10 am to 6 pm, 27th March to 30th September daily except Friday. Telephone: 01732 811145.

❸ Cross the road, then take a broad path between fences to a gate. Go through this, then walk ahead, first along a woodland path, then a field headland for 450 yards. Where the woodland on your right ends, turn right over a stile. Walk down to the far left-hand corner of a field. Cross a stile. Turn left and walk along a road for 200 yards. Turn right over a stile beside a wooden fingerpost signed to Shipbourne.

❹ The footpath now follows a diversion across pasture in Fairlawne Park so, using the tall yellow waymarkers, go ahead to the first marker, then bear right. Leave to your left a fenced stand of young chestnut trees, then a stand of six older ones. Cross a stile and walk ahead to a marker post, then bear left to a post in the fence. Go ahead to the next marker leaving a small oak just to your right. Bear left to reach the next marker then turn right to reach a stile.

❺ Walk down a slope to a metalled driveway above a pond. Turn left. When the driveway swings left, bear right and continue beside a small lake. Go through a gate. Cross a field to a stile and stock-proof bridge over a stream. Walk uphill. Cross a stile, then go between gardens to a small road. Bear right. Turn right, and right again to follow the road across Shipbourne Common to St Giles' church and the Chaser Inn.

Walk 10

The King's Fancy – Anne Boleyn at Hever

Length: 3 or 5¹/₂ miles

Hever Castle

HOW TO GET THERE: Hever lies 10 miles west of Tonbridge and 3 miles east of Edenbridge. Follow the road signed to Hever at the junction of the B269 and the B2027. This runs west from the railway bridge at Bough Beech.

PARKING: There is parking for patrons opposite the King Henry VIII pub. Visitors to Hever may park opposite the entrance to the castle.

MAPS: OS Explorer 147; OS Landranger 188 Maidstone & the Weald (GR 474448).

Introduction

In 1522, Sir Thomas Bullen, newly returned from France where he had been Ambassador for four years, still had great ambitions for himself and his family. For

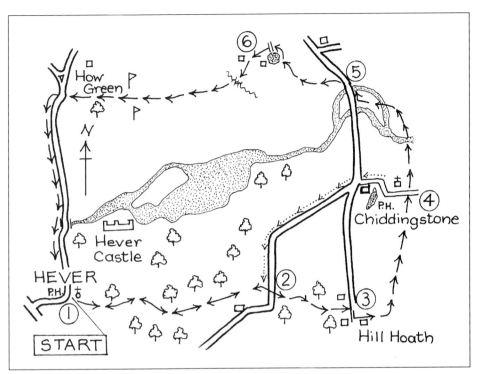

his daughter, Anne, these plans were to go tragically wrong. A beautiful walk from the little village of Hever, where Anne Bullen, or Boleyn, as she came to be known, grew up, and which can be combined with a visit to her father's castle. A woodland path takes you to Chiddingstone, half-timbered houses and sandstone church all stretched along one short road. Then you return, either along a shorter route by a quiet country lane and back through the same woodland as before, or by a longer route, down to the River Eden and up, across fields and along a parkland golf course. Either way you have lovely views.

History

When Anne returned from Paris she was pleased to be chosen to attend Queen Catherine as her lady-in-waiting. Life at her father's country home at Hever was dull for a young woman of 22, compared with diplomatic and court life. No doubt she would have stayed with the Queen for some time had she not fallen in love with Lord Henry Percy. The king observed the infatuation and was not pleased. Sent back to Hever, then, for a while, abroad, Anne soon found her suitor to be Henry VIII himself.

He, tired of Catherine who was unable to provide a male heir, began proceedings to have his first marriage annulled. Henry and Anne were married in January 1533, at first in secret. Their union was announced at Easter that year. Archbishop Cranmer annulled Henry's marriage to Catherine of Aragon and Anne's child, Elizabeth, was

The entrance gate to the castle

born in September. Anne had a miscarriage the next year. Her next child was still-born. Henry had Anne committed to the Tower on a charge of adultery and she was beheaded on 19th May 1536, eleven days before Henry married for the third time.

THE PLACE

When Sir Thomas Bullen inherited Hever Castle, with its impressive 13th-century gatehouse and moat, he built within the walls a spacious dwelling where today you can see reminders of his daughter, Anne including some of her letters to Henry and the prayer book she carried to her execution. Open daily from 1st March to 30th November, 12 noon to 5 pm. Gardens open at 11 am. Telephone: 01732 865224.

THE WALK

❶ Enter St Peter's churchyard and walk to the far side. Turn right, then left, and go down to a footbridge. Cross, then continue along a path with a field to your right. Bear right, cross a footbridge and continue through woodland. When you emerge from the woodland follow a grass verge beside a metalled track. Go through a gate then bear right, across the track. Walk along the right-hand field edge. Go through woodland and continue ahead to a road.

❷ Cross the road. Cross a stile and follow a path between a field and a shaw (a shelter belt of trees). Turn right over a stile, then follow the path down to a stock-proof bridge.

Cross. Walk uphill between coppiced chestnut trees. Cross a stile. Turn right and walk for 20 yards. Turn left. Walk between fences then go down a deep cutting. Go through a swing gate, then continue along a gravel track. Turn right at a T-junction and walk along a rough metalled track.

❸ Pass Hill Hoath House, then turn left into a farm yard. Walk beside the left-hand fence. Cross a stile and continue until you meet a fence ahead of you. Here cross a stile to your left, then bear right uphill across a large field to a stile at the left-hand end of a short hedgeline. Follow the path into Chiddingstone village.

❹ For the shorter walk, turn left into the centre of Chiddingstone. Turn right by the Castle Inn and follow the road to crossroads. Go ahead, uphill, bearing left twice, to return to 2. Now retrace your steps to Hever.

> **HOSTELRY AND THIRSTQUENCHER**
>
> At the King Henry VIII, opposite St Peter's church, you will find traditional meals well served, and Shepherd Neame ales. The inn is open from 11 am to 11 pm. Food is served from 12 noon to 2.30 pm and from 6.30 pm to 9 pm. In winter it is closed between 2.30 pm and 4.30 pm. Telephone: 01732 862457. In Chiddingstone you will find the 15th-century Castle Inn. Telephone: 01892 870326.

> **OTHER PLACES OF INTEREST**
>
> It is worth lingering in the medieval village of Chiddingstone. At Chiddingstone Castle you can see some fine art treasures, and wood panelling said to have come from Anne Boleyn's own bedstead. Telephone 01892 870347.

To continue the full walk, turn right in Chiddingstone. After 50 yards turn left. Follow the footpath downhill to the River Eden. Cross a bridge and continue ahead uphill. Pass houses at Somerden Green, then walk uphill for $1/2$ mile. Turn left over a stile set to face your path, at the end of a line of trees. Cross a field, bearing slightly to your right, between two oaks. Cross a stock-proof bridge over an ox-bow loop of the River Eden. Cross a field, keeping to the right of an old hedge line. Cross a stile then turn right along a road for 250 yards.

❺ Bear left into a field. Follow the headland leaving the hedge to your left. After 260 yards turn left through a gap in the hedge, then turn immediately right. Continue along a headland with a hedge to your right. Go through a gateway. Bear left along the headland, with the hedge on your left. Continue past farm buildings. Turn left down a narrow path to a stile. Cross a lane. Cross a stile into a field, then take the alternative route to your left along the headland.

❻ Cross a stile onto a golf course. Bear left round the back of a hut and follow the car track downhill. At cross-tracks turn left then follow a gravel track round to your right, crossing a stream. Continue first between trees, then above the golf course. Where the gravel track turns right to the Club House, continue ahead. Cross a stile and follow a grass track between trees. Cross a stile. Turn left to follow the road back to Hever for $3/4$ mile.

WALK 11
VISIONARY AND A PAWN – THE HOLY MAID OF
KENT AT ALDINGTON

Length: 4¹/₂ miles

The deserted chapel at Court-at-Street

HOW TO GET THERE: Aldington Corner lies 3¹/₂ miles north-west of Lympne, 1 mile from the B2067.

PARKING: There is parking beside the Walnut Tree Inn for patrons. You can also park along the roadside.

MAPS: OS Explorer 137; OS Landranger 189 Ashford & Romney Marsh (GR 063365; the chapel 090351).

INTRODUCTION

The sad heroine of this chapter is Elizabeth Barton, who made her name as a visionary in the reign of Henry VIII and later became known as the Holy Maid of Kent. Wide

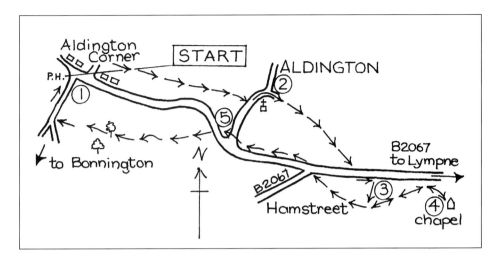

fields and wonderful views mark this walk from Aldington Corner to the deserted chapel at Court-at-Street near Lympne, where the Holy Maid of Kent first became famous in the reign of Henry VIII. You pass St Martin's church, Aldington, and then the site of the long-vanished Archbishop's palace. Stunning views over Romney Marsh unfold, with Dungeness and its shingle bank to the east, the Hastings cliffs to the west. To reach the chapel the walk follows the ancient cliff line, then returns below the woods of Aldington Knoll.

History

It was sometime in 1526 that the young Elizabeth Barton went to live in a chapel set high on the old cliff line above Romney Marsh. As a servant girl in the house of Thomas Cobb, who was bailiff of Archbishop Warham's estates at Aldington, she had had a seizure during a long illness, in the course of which she foretold the death of a child. Then she claimed to have had a vision in which the Virgin Mary told her that, if she visited a chapel a few miles away, she would be cured. The strange story was brought to the attention of the Archbishop and he gave her the permission she needed to make the visit. Elizabeth went to the chapel and recovered from her illness. She stayed on there but her ecstatic utterances continued. She became known as the Holy Maid of Kent and a stream of pilgrims began to visit the isolated spot.

The Archbishop recommended that she become a nun in the convent of St Sepulchre in Canterbury. There she was unwittingly embroiled in politics and denounced Henry VIII's plans to divorce Catherine of Aragon. After Henry had married Anne Boleyn she became even more impassioned. The King naturally was not amused. Elizabeth was tried in London for treason in 1533, and executed at Tyburn in 1535.

The Place

The simple ragstone chapel at Court-at-Street may have first fallen into decay in the late 15th or early 16th century. Briefly restored when Elizabeth Barton made it famous, it still has the outline of its late Perpendicular doorway. Its main interest today lies in its history and the marvellous view from the slopes beside it.

THE WALK

❶ Turn left outside the Walnut Tree Inn and cross the main road. Turn right. Turn left into Goldwell Lane. After 200 yards turn right through a gate then follow the headland towards St Martin's, Aldington, whose tower you see on the skyline. Cross a stile at the bottom of the field. Follow a path between

Aldington's smuggling past seen on the pub sign at Aldington Corner

hedge lines. Continue ahead up the field, now aiming to leave the church tower just to your left. Join a concrete farm track to reach the road. Turn left. Cor.tinue for 200 yards past the church. A visit to St Martin's church is recommended if it is open. The earliest parts date from the 12th century. There are some beautiful 14th century choir stalls and it has one of the finest Perpendicular-style church towers in England.

❷ Bear right up a gravel drive opposite Street Farm and make for the right hand of two gates ahead of you. When you reach two small houses bear right over the ground which is thought to be the site of the old archbishop's palace and walk to a gate in the fence ahead. Follow the yellow arrow ahead through woodland. Walk alongside a fence on your left above a field for 100 yards. At the corner of the field below you bear right and walk across a large field, going slightly uphill. As you rise, aim for a single telegraph pole, set to the left of others. Continue on this line to a road. Turn left along the B2067. This can be busy at times so walk carefully along the verge for 200 yards.

❸ Just after a bend in the road turn right. Follow a broad farm track to a gate. Go through this, then continue, downhill, to a stile on your left. Cross this stile and walk along a grass path under the old cliff. Cross a stile, then continue, with a fence on your right. Just before a gate turn right over a stile and follow a path through woodland until you reach open hillside. Make for the stone building ahead. This is the chapel Elizabeth Barton once made famous.

❹ Retrace your steps to the woodland and follow the path back to two stiles. Cross the left-hand stile then walk back under the cliff line. After the second stile, ignore the right turn by which you arrived and continue ahead. Cross a stile and walk along a field path, leaving woodland to your left. Go through a gate to the right of a garden and continue up to the road. Cross the B2067 and take the road ahead towards Aldington. Continue past the right-hand turn to St Martin's church.

❺ After 200 yards turn left across the road. Go through a gateway opposite a farm entrance. Walk ahead to a gap in a fence, then go ahead to a gateway. Bear right and go to the right of the taller of two pylons. Make for trees below you and cross a bridge over a small ghyll or stream. Turn left and walk to a stile in the fence ahead. Turn right just before the stile and walk uphill. Cross a stile. Bear left and walk with a fence to your right. Cross a stile and walk uphill towards a marker post. Turn left, then right, over a stile. Go ahead to a stile. Cross, then turn right up the road to return to the Walnut Tree Inn.

HOSTELRY AND THIRSTQUENCHER

The Walnut Tree Inn, at Aldington Corner, first built around 1240 and a favourite haunt of the Aldington Gang of smugglers, combines history and a warm welcome. You will enjoy their local fish, game, and home-made steak and kidney pie, and Shepherd Neame ales. It is normally closed on Monday but a group may book ahead for that day. Telephone: 01233 720298.

OTHER PLACES OF INTEREST

As a contrast after this melancholy story you can visit John Aspinall's Wild Life Park at Port Lympne, set on the slopes above Romney Marsh. Open daily, except Christmas Day, from 10 am to dusk. Telephone: 01303 264647.

WALK 12
BROADCLOTH HEYDAY – QUEEN ELIZABETH I VISITS CRANBROOK

Length: 4¹/₂ miles

Cranbrook

HOW TO GET THERE: Sissinghurst lies on the A262, ³/₄ mile east of the A229 and 4 miles west of the A274 at Biddenden.

PARKING: There is parking for patrons beside the Bull Inn at Sissinghurst.

MAPS: OS Explorer 136; OS Landranger 188 Maidstone & the Weald (GR 795376; Cranbrook 776361).

INTRODUCTION

The export market brought Cranbrook a reputation coveted by many. Sheep, or rather, their fleece provided the key to this success and in the late Middle Ages and in Tudor times the Wealden town of Cranbrook was as prosperous as any. On this walk you start from the village of Sissinghurst then walk to Cranbrook over slopes once

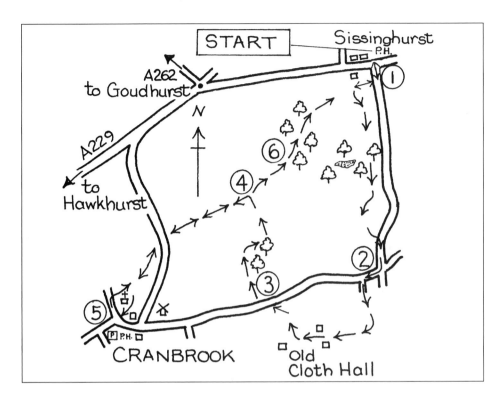

grazed by those sheep. You see the streams beside which local people turned the wool into the fine broadcloth that brought them fame. On your way you pass near two of the old Cloth Halls where the cloth was checked and stored. In Cranbrook itself you can explore a town which still carries the air of dignity first cultivated 600 years ago.

HISTORY

1573 remained for long in the minds of the people of Cranbrook, for in that year Queen Elizabeth I came to celebrate new trade deals for their cloth. Alighting from her carriage outside the Cloth Hall, now the George Hotel, she walked over red cloth to inspect the broadcloth made inside. A new peal of bells rang loudly nearby in her honour and the people's pride in their success knew no bounds.

From the time in 1331 that Edward III forbade the sale of wool abroad and invited Flemish weavers to work in England, Cranbrook's fortunes flourished. John Kemp, weaver, settled nearby and, utilising water from the many local streams, he revolutionised the fulling process. From then on, in the late Middle Ages and in Tudor times, the countryside resounded to the sound of hammers as fullers pounded the broadcloth to the fine texture for which the area became famous. By 1400 the new industry was firmly established. Production of broadcloth had increased three-fold, exports had risen nine-fold. At the height of its success, Cranbrook produced more

St Dunstan's church, Cranbrook

than 100,000 bales a year. The town was one of the most prosperous in Kent.

THE PLACE
With its half-timbered houses and narrow streets, Cranbrook retains much of the style that set it apart in the Middle Ages and Tudor times. St Dunstan's church, sometimes called the 'Cathedral of the Weald', is a magnificent sandstone church built from the mid-14th century, with money from the cloth trade. The Cranbrook Museum tells you the full history of the area and is open from 2 pm to 4.30 pm: in March, October and November on Wednesday, Thursday and Saturday; from April to September on Tuesday to Saturday. Telephone: 01580 712368.

THE WALK
❶ Take the road opposite the Bull, signed to Benenden and Iden Green. Turn right after the first set of houses and follow the footpath until you reach cross-tracks. Turn left and walk downhill, following the headland of a large field and leaving a fence on your left. At the bottom of the field follow the path through woodland, crossing three bridges. Cross a stile into a field. Turn right towards a fence, then left, and follow the field edge, leaving the fence to your right. Turn left at the field corner and make for a stile to the left of a gate. Turn right and walk along a road.

❷ At cross-roads turn right, then take the first turning on your left. Continue ahead as the lane becomes a path, first grass, then of earth. Just past a small bridge turn right and walk up a field headland with trees to your right. As the trees thin out, bear left uphill. Leave a solitary tree to your right and aim to the right of four poplars which grow to the right of converted farm buildings. When you reach a metalled lane bear right. Walk between houses at Coursehorne Farm, then follow the lane past the Old Cloth Hall for 3/4 mile to the road.

❸ Cross the road and turn left. After 100 yards turn right. Cross a stile, then bear left to the far left-hand corner of the field. Follow the path between trees. Turn right and follow the field headland with woodland to your right. Enter woodland, then bear right over a stock-proof bridge. Walk uphill leaving a line of willows to your right and make for the corner of woodland ahead to your right. Turn right and walk to the field boundary. Turn left and walk to the top of the field. Cross a stile and turn left.

❹ Walk to a stile, cross it and continue to a road. Cross the road to a playing field, taking steps down and up. Cross the field, then, opposite a children's play-area, turn left into the churchyard. Follow the path ahead. Turn right to go round the church, then go down steps to reach the town centre at the junction of Stone Street and High Street. Take time now to explore this lovely old town.

❺ When you are ready to continue, return to the place where you ended **4**. Turn right into Carriers Road. Walk for 100 yards. Turn right and walk up a broad metalled area to reach the playing field. Return across the field to the road. Cross the road then retrace your steps along the lane. Cross the stile ahead of you. Ignoring the stile you crossed from the field at **4,** go ahead along a concrete farm track. Where the farm track bears right, continue ahead. Cross a stile into woodland.

❻ Walk along a broad track through the woodland and go downhill to a field bridge and stile. Walk ahead up the field to a stile. Take care as you cross this stile as there is a steep drop down on the other side. Cross a metalled track. Go up steps and continue along a lane, between hedges. When you emerge into an open field go ahead, leaving a hedge to your left. Continue first along a field headland, then along a lane beside the field. Go ahead at cross-tracks to rejoin the first lane of your walk. Turn left when you reach the road to return to the Bull.

HOSTELRY AND THIRSTQUENCHER

The Bull at Sissinghurst offers a wide range of excellent home cooked meals, with fine pastas and fish dishes such as mussels, baked cod or grilled salmon. As a free house it offers Harvey's, IPA and Pedigree among other ales. Open all day every day. Telephone: 01580 712821. In Cranbrook you can pause at the George Hotel on the corner of Stone Street. Telephone: 01580 713348.

OTHER PLACES OF INTEREST

Sissinghurst Gardens (National Trust) are open between April and October; telephone: 01580 712580. Drive to Goudhurst and see the collection of keyboard instruments at Finchcocks. Telephone: 01580 211702.

WALK 13

STATESMAN, POET AND SOLDIER – SIR PHILIP
SIDNEY AND PENSHURST

Length: 4 miles

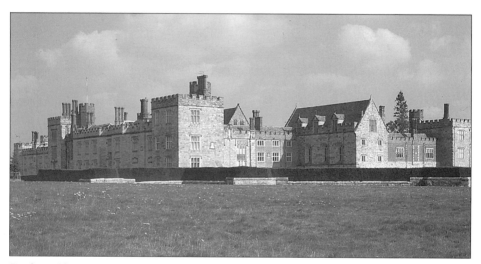

Penshurst Place

HOW TO GET THERE: Turn off the A26 Tonbridge to Tunbridge Wells road, and follow the B2176 to Penshurst or take the B2188 south from the B2027 just west of Leigh.

PARKING: There is parking for patrons behind the Leicester Arms. To reach the car park for visitors to Penshurst Place go through the archway to the east of the village and follow the signs.

MAPS: OS Explorer 147; OS Landranger 188 Maidstone & the Weald (GR 527438).

INTRODUCTION

'Your need is greater than mine': so the dying Sir Philip Sidney is reported to have said as he gave water intended for him to another injured soldier. Penshurst Place was the home of Sir Philip Sidney, who brought poetry to new heights in the time of Queen Elizabeth I, and who in death became the romantic ideal admired by all. This fine

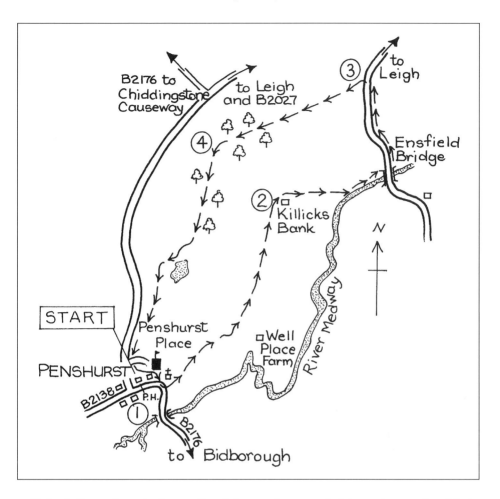

walk leads through part of a medieval deer park, converted to pasture and arable in the 18th century, down to the River Medway, clear and fairly fast-moving. Back on higher ground, you look down over the parkland of Penshurst estate before returning to Penshurst village.

HISTORY

Under Elizabeth I the last years of the 16th century proved happier for England than its beginning. Religious strife and troubles over the royal succession had faded to give way to an age often called 'golden'. The death of Sir Philip Sidney in 1586 marked an important point in those years.

Philip had followed his father as statesman and soldier but he also showed remarkable ability in languages and literature. His early years as a young man at Elizabeth's court, and at his father's home at Penshurst, were rich years for him in

The Leicester coat of arms on the wall of Penshurst church

many ways. He corresponded with foreign statesmen and entertained them. He took great interest in the discoveries of Raleigh and Drake. He discussed topics ranging from art to chemistry. He revelled in sports and athletic contests. He wrote sonnets, literary criticism and a fine prose romance, *Arcadia*. Sidney wrote only for friends, never for publication. Then, not quite 32 years old, he died a soldier's death fighting against the Spanish in the Netherlands. He was buried in St Paul's Cathedral. The praise and adulation for this ideal of gentlemanly virtue knew no bounds.

The Place

You can see the helmet Sir Philip Sidney wore in battle in the Great Hall of his family home at Penshurst Place, one of the finest houses in Kent. Penshurst Place grew over the centuries. Sir Henry, Philip's father, added parts in Elizabethan times. The next owner surrounded the manor house with the walls and battlements you see today. But it is the Great Hall, built by Robert Hurley in the 14th century, whose style and vast dimensions still amaze. Open daily from the end of March to the end of October, from 12 noon to 6 pm. Grounds open from 11 am. Telephone: 01892 870307.

The Walk

❶ Turn right outside the Leicester Arms and walk along the road. Leave Leicester Square to your left. Where the road turns right, go ahead through the large archway at the entrance to Penshurst Place and walk along a metalled track. Pass a small lake and continue for 500 yards. Turn left through a squeeze gate which you will find to the right of a metal gate. Immediately turn right and walk up the right-hand side of the field. Go through a gate. Bear left and walk to a post at the top of a field. At the post continue ahead to a stile. Cross the stile then walk along the headland of a field, leaving a fence to your right. Continue ahead along a concrete farm track.

❷ At a gate at Killicks Bank bear right over a stile. Cross a concrete farm track. Cross a stile into a field and bear right to a marker post. Go down the slope and cross a stock-proof bridge. Cross a field to the River Medway. Turn left and continue beside the river to Enfield Bridge, a haven for wildlife. Go through a squeeze gate onto the road. Turn left and walk carefully along the road for $1/2$ mile, going uphill.

❸ At the top of the slope turn left at Pauls Hill House. Walk up a rough track leaving the house to your left. Cross a stile into a field. Walk to the far right-hand corner, then turn left. At the corner of the field turn right and cross a stile beside a gate. Continue along a grassy track between trees. Go through a squeeze gate and continue along a broad avenue lined with plane trees.

❹ Follow the track as it bears left and leads downhill. You now see Penshurst Place in the parkland below you. Go through a squeeze gate halfway down the slope and walk ahead. Turn right through a gate set beside a metal gate just below a fenced, old oak. Follow the path beside a fence above a lake. Where the fence bears left round a lake go ahead through a gate. Leave a gnarled oak on your right. At least 400 years old, this oak was already growing at the time of Sir Philip's birth in 1554. Now walk to the main driveway for Penshurst Place. Cross this going though squeeze gates on either side of the drive. Bear right to a stile in the fence by the road, then bear left and follow the trodden path across the field to the far right-hand side, making for the church of St John the Evangelist, to the right of Penshurst Place. Go into the churchyard, skirt the church and walk under the arch into Leicester Square. Turn right along the road to return to the Leicester Arms.

HOSTELRY AND THIRSTQUENCHER

At the Leicester Arms, named in honour of Sir Philip's brother who became Earl of Leicester in 1618, you can choose local Larkin's ale or London Pride, Larkin's Porter in winter or Adnam's Best in summer. At the bar you find curry or T-bone steak, chicken korma and pan-fried pork, while fish dishes figure in the restaurant. Open all day every day. Telephone: 01892 870551.

OTHER PLACES OF INTEREST

Groombridge Place, 5 miles south on the B2110, is a 17th-century manor house, surrounded by a moat. You can see the walled garden which John Evelyn, the diarist and horticulturist, helped to design. You can also see a sanctuary for birds of prey and an Enchanted Forest, created in the wooded slopes above the house. Telephone: 01892 863999.

WALK 14

A COUNTY AT WAR WITH ITSELF – THE DERING FAMILY OF PLUCKLEY

Length: 4 miles

Oasts at Malmains

HOW TO GET THERE: Pluckley lies 3 miles south of the A20 at Charing, on the Charing-Smarden road.

PARKING: There is sometimes space in the village square outside the Black Horse. Patrons may park in the car park behind the Black Horse, reached from the main road.

MAPS: OS Explorer 137; OS Landranger 189: Ashford & Romney Marsh (GR 926455).

INTRODUCTION

In 1660 Charles II's return from exile brought great excitement to the whole county of Kent. Along Charles' route from Dover to London bystanders danced and threw garlands. In Pluckley people had their own reason to rejoice. For the Lord of the

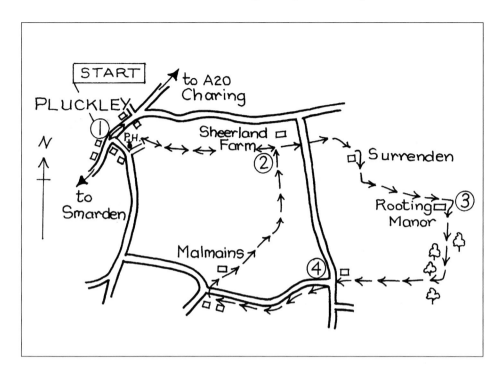

Manor, Sir Edward Dering, had been returned as knight of the shire and MP. The Dering family's position, undermined during the Civil War, was finally restored. Normality had returned to the village. This walk takes you over land once owned by the Dering family, through orchards and past what remains of the Derings' home, Surrenden Dering. You pass two other old manor houses, Rooting Manor, mentioned in Domesday Book, and Malmains. Almost all the time you have wonderful views through the fruit trees to the High Weald.

History

The Civil War brought perplexing and troubled times for the people of Kent. While the rest of England seemed to be divided between Cavaliers and Roundheads, Kent also contained moderates who believed their main duty lay above all with their own people. Sir Edward Dering, the first baronet and MP for Kent since 1625, had been one of these. Well-educated and an exceptional man of letters, he favoured both constitution and king. At first a keen supporter of parliament, he grew to dislike its extremism. He raised his own regiment and fought for King Charles at the Battle of Edgehill. Then, rejecting the cavaliers' excesses, and a sick man, he returned to his wife and family only to find that in his absence the Roundheads had plundered his home and estate. He spent his last months in poverty in a farmhouse on the estate and died in 1644.

St Nicholas church

His son, the second Sir Edward, did what he could during the years of Cromwell's rule but only the Restoration of 1660 gave him full scope to follow his father's traditional role. Sir Edward's diary entry for 1st May 1660 struck a cheerful note: 'This day began the happy worke of our restitution to our ancient lawes.'

THE PLACE
The village of Pluckley clusters around the tiny square outside the Black Horse. Here as everywhere are the arched windows introduced by a later Dering to celebrate another occasion during the Civil War, when the younger Sir Edward, so tells the tale, escaped through such a window when fleeing more Roundheads. St Nicholas' church with broach spire dominates the far end of the village. Much of Surrenden Dering was destroyed by fire in 1952 but you can see a clock tower above the trees.

THE WALK
❶ Walk from the village square to the main road. Turn right and walk up the road for 100 yards. Turn right and walk past into the entrance to the Black Horse car park, going ahead through a swing gate. Cross a field to a gap in the hedge, 50 yards from the

far right-hand corner. Walk ahead through orchards. Pass Sheerland House. Cross a metalled track leading into Sheerland Farm.

❷ Continue ahead along a broad track to a metalled lane. Cross the lane, then take the footpath ahead, leaving a high wall to your left. Cross a stile. Bear right across a field towards the far right-hand corner. Go through a metal swing gate and turn left. From here you can see the old clock tower of Surrenden Dering above the trees. Follow a farm track for 130 yards then bear right into an orchard. Walk towards fruit trees. Turn right following a white arrow and walk between trees to a broad clearing. Turn left and continue down a broad path to a windbreak. Twenty yards after the windbreak bear right along a path between fruit trees and yellow markers. At the end turn right along a broad grass track. Go into a field beyond the orchard. Turn right along the headland, then left, leaving the fence to your right.

❸ Just past a metal gate turn right over a stile and walk down a verge to a metalled drive. Turn right, then almost immediately left, to follow the drive past Rooting Manor. Continue along a wide track into a field. You now leave a low stone wall to your right, with a small woodland area beyond. Continue until you reach woodland ahead of you. Turn right along a farm track. Once past trees continue along a broad track between fields. When the main track turns left, go ahead along a field headland following a blue marker and leaving a fence on your left. Continue through two swing gates and walk over gravel, through a garden, leaving a house to your right, to reach a road.

❹ Turn right, then left and follow a road for $1/2$ mile. Immediately opposite a house turn right and cross a stile. Walk up two fields, crossing a stile between them. Malmains is over to your left. Cross a stile in the right-hand corner of the second field and continue on the same line, going gently uphill, with fruit trees to your left and a windbreak to your right. Continue uphill along a metalled track. At Sheerland Farm, turn left and retrace your tracks to the road just above Pluckley village. Turn left, then left again, to reach the village square.

WALK 15

A FLEET ON FIRE – THE ANGLO-DUTCH WAR COMES TO UPNOR CASTLE

Length: 2 miles

Gun emplacements at Upnor Castle

HOW TO GET THERE: From the junction of the A2/M2 take the A289 to the junction with the A228. At the first roundabout go ahead as for Strood and Rochester. Turn left at the next roundabout, signed to Chatham Maritime, then first left to Upnor. Turn first right and follow the English Heritage sign.

PARKING: You will find a car park to your right as you approach the top of the village.

MAPS: OS Explorer 163; OS Landranger 178 The Thames Estuary (GR 757706).

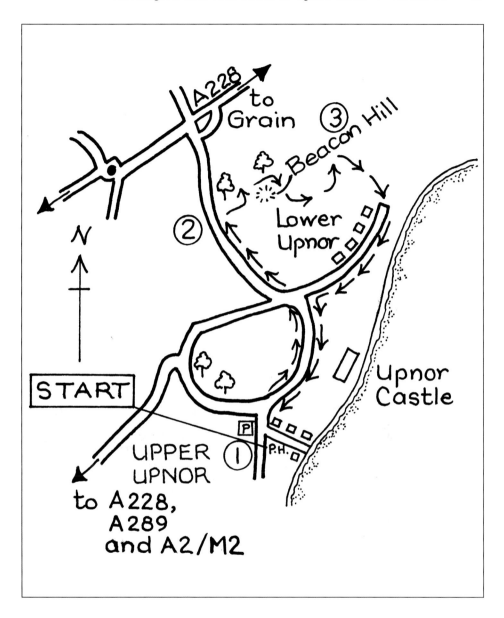

INTRODUCTION

The tiny village of Upnor, near Rochester, provides the setting for a walk with a maritime flavour. From Upper Upnor, with its single street leading down to the River Medway and its ragstone castle beside the water, you walk to Beacon Hill and enjoy an outstanding view as the estuary unfolds towards Sheerness and the mouth of the Thames, before returning beside the river. The scene will be calm today, with modern sailing craft scattered on the waters of the Medway, but here you can relive the terrifying moments when the small garrison at Upnor Castle saw the precious English fleet destroyed before its eyes.

HISTORY

The waters of the Medway were believed to be ideal for the protection of shipping and in the 16th century Queen Elizabeth's fleet frequently used the waters downstream from Rochester Bridge as an anchorage. Upnor Castle was built between 1559 and 1567 as a bulwark to protect that fleet but, in all the hundred years since its construction, Upnor Castle had seen no action. Now England was at war with Holland over commercial interests. Suddenly in June 1667, the small force garrisoned there saw the skyline around Sheerness on the Isle of Sheppey ablaze with fire and the men feared what only a few days before they had thought impossible. In the time it took for reinforcements to arrive, the Dutch sailed up the river. They took the flagship, *The Royal Charles*, and set fire to many other ships before the English were able to set up artillery beside Upnor Castle and bombard the enemy until they retreated. The destruction and humiliation were hard to bear. A stronger fort was built at Sheerness, two more forts were built downstream and Upnor, no longer of use as a fort, became a place for storage.

THE PLACE

A visit to Upnor Castle, now owned by English Heritage, is a must, for its situation as well as its history. The battery overlooking the river, the audio-tour and the interactive displays inside will soon reveal just how close the place was to the enemy fire and evoke the terrifying moments of the Dutch attack. Upnor Castle stands just north of the view-point at the bottom of the High Street, Upnor's delightful only street. Open 1st April to 30th September. Telephone: 01634 827980/718742.

THE WALK

❶ Outside the King's Arms cross the top of the High Street and follow Upchat Road as it bears left to a junction of four ways. Cross and take the road ahead. Walk up the right-hand side of the road, then follow the footpath above a quarry which lies below you on your right.

❷ Turn right at the end of the quarry fencing, and follow the path into woodland. Cross a stile and walk uphill

HOSTELRY AND THIRSTQUENCHER

You will receive a warm welcome at the King's Arms at the top of the High Street in Upper Upnor. Ales include Courage Best, Old Peculier and Masterbrew along with a great selection of local ales, such as Friggin the Riggin from Chatham Dockyard across the river. Pies made on the spot are a speciality. Sunday lunch will set you up for the week while the evening à la carte offers a wide range from steaks to lobster. In winter there is a roaring log fire. Telephone: 01634 717490.

Upnor Castle seen from the village

with the fencing to your right. Where the quarry appears to end take two steps to your right, then continue ahead uphill, still beside good fencing. Beware of small, low stumps as you follow the earth path. Turn left at the top of the wiring and follow the path along the level, then turn right, always keeping between fences. The path turns to grass as you continue uphill. Cross a broad track, leaving a large metal gate to your right. Continue ahead following a narrow path beside fencing, going steadily downhill. Turn left over a stile.

> **OTHER PLACES OF INTEREST**
>
> Easily accessible now from Upnor, with the Medway Tunnel, the Dockyard at Chatham Maritime is a fascinating place. It tells the history of the Navy on this site from the time of Henry VIII, when storehouses were first rented to service the fleet at anchor in the Medway. The first warship launched here joined the fleet to confront the Armada. The first 'Ironclad' was made here too. Telephone: 01634 812551.

Continue to a stile leading into the corner of an expanse of open space which slopes uphill and ahead of you.

❸ Turn left and walk uphill to a seat in the corner of the open space from where you have that wonderful view over the Medway. To continue, retrace your tracks for just over 100 yards, then bear slightly left and follow the path down the centre of a small gully. When you reach trees at the bottom of the field take a path into woodland. Follow this downhill and join the road-end in Lower Upnor beside a Venture Playground. Turn right and walk beside the Medway along Upnor Road. Cross the road just past the beginning of the Barracks wall. Go up the steps ahead and walk back to the King's Arms.

WALK 16

FOR FEAR OF NAPOLEON – THE ROYAL MILITARY CANAL AT STONE-IN-OXNEY

Length: 2 miles

A view of the canal

HOW TO GET THERE: Stone-in-Oxney is 2 miles south-west of Appledore, midway between the B2080 Tenterden-Appledore and B2082 Tenterden-Rye roads.

PARKING: There is parking beside the Crown Inn for patrons.

MAPS: OS Explorer 125; OS Landranger 189 Ashford & Romney Marsh (GR 939278; Stone Bridge 946265).

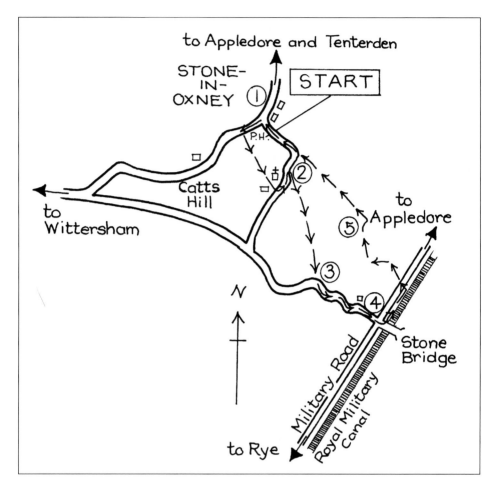

INTRODUCTION

Never had there been a threat like it. The name Napoleon Bonaparte struck fear into everyone. A strange monument to that fear can be seen in the Royal Military Canal which runs beside Romney and Walland Marshes, and the small village of Stone-in-Oxney makes the starting point for an intriguing walk. From a gentle slope up to the church of St Mary, you continue across fields with views over the wide expanse of the Marsh, then walk down to the canal for a closer look at this most unusual of defence works. You then return by fields to the peaceful village.

HISTORY

In 1803, after a brief respite, Britain declared war against Napoleon and France for the second time in 10 years. William Pitt, recalled from retirement to be Prime Minister once more, knew that the country's safety depended on a new approach to its defence. Romney Marsh lay close to Napoleon's forces, who were massing across the English Channel little more than 20 miles away. Low-lying and flat, it appeared a weak area for defence. Pitt soon outlined a plan – to build a line of Martello Towers along the coast and to excavate a defensive canal behind the Kent marshes, beneath the old cliff line. If both of these failed to deter the French army, the marshland itself would be flooded. Work began in October 1804. The canal was filled with water in August 1806. Mocked by many as foolish beyond belief, its effectiveness was never put to the test, for Napoleon never invaded. The Royal Military Canal was opened for public navigation in 1810.

HOSTELRY AND THIRSTQUENCHER

Friendly and cosy, the Crown Inn offers Masterbrew, Otter Bitter and Canterbury Jack among other ales. The house steak and ale pie and the confit of duck are both winners. Open Monday 12 noon to 3 pm (no food), Tuesday to Saturday 12 noon to 3 pm and 6 pm to 11 pm, Sundays 12 noon to 5 pm. Telephone: 01233 758789. There are also several good pubs and tea houses in Appledore.

OTHER PLACES OF INTEREST

The bull carved on the stone block beneath the tower in St Mary's church, Stone-in-Oxney, suggests it is an altar from a Roman Mithraeum. Found beneath the church in the early 18th century, it was used as a mounting block for many years. At Appledore you will find another attractive stretch of the canal.

THE PLACE

The canal runs for 28 miles between Cliff End and Hythe. For the most part it runs in straight stretches, with a bend, or *enfilade*, every 650 yards. This *enfilade* enabled a gun emplacement to provide gun-fire from both sides should the enemy try to cross. Beside the canal is a parapet, formed from the earth thrown up during excavation. You can see the quarters built for officers at Iden Lock, at the junction of the Military Road and the A268, south of Stone Bridge. The canal is now a haven for wild life.

THE WALK

❶ Turn left outside the Crown Inn and walk along Catt's Lane. After 300 yards, turn left and walk along a lane between a fence and a hedge. Follow the path round the end of a garden, then up a gentle slope, through woodland to a gate. Go through the gate, then walk up a grassy path towards St Mary's church. Cross a stile, then, following the arrow on the stile, bear right down to a field bridge in a hollow. Bear left, up the slope towards the church. Cross a stile into the churchyard. Go ahead, round the west end of the church, to the road.

❷ Turn left. After 75 yards, turn right over a stile. Bear right and walk to the right-hand corner of the field. Cross a stile to the left of a gate. Go down a slope to your left, then turn right and go along the headland of the field, leaving the fence above you on your right. Continue as the field opens into a larger field, pausing of course, to enjoy that view. Walk down the slope. Cross a tree-lined ghyll or stream. Cross a stile and

Looking towards Romney Marsh from Stone-in-Oxney

walk uphill with the hedge on your right. Cross a stile in the right-hand corner of the field. Continue ahead to a lane, crossing two more stiles. Then walk 25 yards to a narrow road.

❸ Turn left. Walk down to the Military Road. Cross the road and go ahead along a gravel lane for 20 yards. Just before Stone Bridge turn left over a stile.

❹ Walk with the Royal Military Canal to your right for ¼ mile. Turn left and cross a stile leading down to the Military Road. Turn right and walk until level with a wooden finger post set on the far bank of a dyke. Cross the road. Walk down the slope and cross a stock-proof bridge. Turn half-right and walk to a yellow marker post beside a small dyke. Turn left and walk to a stile beside a gate by trees where the hedge line comes towards you. Turn half-right. Walk to a wooden bridge over a large dyke. Cross this and continue towards the far left-hand corner of the field.

❺ Just before the field corner, cross a stile then turn right and walk to the corner of the field you have just left. Bear left and walk uphill towards the right-hand corner of the field. Go to the left of a large hawthorn. Cross a stile. Bear slightly left towards a telegraph pole, then go down a very steep slope to a stile in the hedge. Cross the stile, taking care because there is a steep flight of steps on the far side. Turn right and walk down the road. You will reach the Crown Inn after 500 yards.

WALK 17

NINETEENTH-CENTURY SMUGGLERS – A TIME OF LAWLESSNESS IN RUCKINGE

Length: 2¹/₂ miles

The Ransley Memorial, Ruckinge

HOW TO GET THERE: Ruckinge lies on the B2067, 2 miles east of Hamstreet and 6¹/₂ miles west of Lympne.

PARKING: There is parking for patrons beside the Blue Anchor Inn.

MAPS: OS Explorer 125; OS Landranger 189 Ashford & Romney Marsh (GR 027337).

INTRODUCTION

In the 18th and early 19th centuries Romney Marsh was not a place to be alone at night. Sparsely inhabited, with isolated settlements and a maze of dykes known only

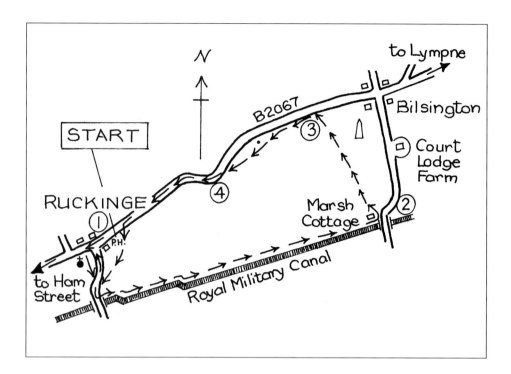

to a few, it offered close-knit bands of smugglers in south-east England an ideal place to run their goods ashore. More than one battle was fought on this lonely space between bandit and preventiveman. On this walk you have the chance to see where one gang of smugglers once plied their trade. From the small village of Ruckinge, just above the Marsh, which provided one of several staging posts for illicit goods, you stroll beside a stretch of the Royal Military Canal to Bilsington, then return to the village across fields and a short bit of road. This is a peaceful area today and the church of St Mary Magdalene has an idyllic situation above Romney Marsh, but you can still find reminders of a lawless past.

History

Monarchs had for centuries taxed exports or imports, so smuggling was a long-established occupation on Romney Marsh. At different times the goods ranged from wines, silk and fashionable clothes to salt, spirits and tobacco. At one time woollen cloth dominated the contraband market, at another, tea, where a smuggler could make a return of up to 400%. Smugglers grouped themselves in well-organised bands and the excisemen were too few to subdue them.

One smuggling gang, based at Aldington, gained a fierce reputation. In 1820 a running battle developed where five men were killed and 25 men injured. In another battle one preventiveman and four smugglers were killed. The gang leader was later

St Mary Magdalene's church

caught and hanged. George Ransley took over as leader of the gang and the smuggling continued unabated. There were further skirmishes and a £500 reward offered for information. In 1826 Ransley was spotted by Bow Street Runners outside the Blue Anchor in Ruckinge. Two gang members turned King's evidence and Ransley was taken in his bed in the early hours one morning. But it could not be proved beyond reasonable doubt that he had committed the crimes. His death sentence was commuted and he was transported to Tasmania.

THE PLACE

The Blue Anchor, built in 1738, was a favourite haunt of the Ransley Gang and other local miscreants. Another reminder of this violent family remains in the peaceful churchyard of St Mary Magdalene, Ruckinge. There you will find a simple wooden plank supported by three iron posts. Once painted and bearing an inscription, it is said to have

HOSTELRY AND THIRSTQUENCHER

The Blue Anchor welcomes families and has an excellent play area and garden. It is open every day of the week and all day on Saturday and Sunday. There is a good range of cask and keg ales and bitters with a wide variety of food on offer. Telephone: 01233 732387.

been erected to William and James Ransley who were hanged in 1800 for smuggling offences.

THE WALK

❶ Turn left as you leave the Blue Anchor. Walk along the road until you reach the gateway leading into the churchyard of St Mary Magdalene. To see the Ransley headboard, turn right, then go ahead past the west end of the church with its fine Norman tympanum over the doorway. The Ransley headboard is ahead to your right. To rejoin the route, return to the church entrance path and follow the public footpath past the east end of the church. Walk down to a stile. Cross and walk ahead beside garden walls. Cross a stile and continue to a yellow-painted walkers' marker post. Bear left to a stile. Cross onto the road, Marsh Lane. Turn right, then left, over a stile, to join the path on the north side of the Royal Military Canal. Now follow the canal-side path for almost a mile, crossing one stile as you go. The canal was built as part of the defences against invasion by Napoleon in the early 1800s (see Walk 16).

❷ Cross a second stile and turn left along the road. Pass Marsh Cottage. As the road swings to your right, turn left down the verge and cross a stile. Then cross a bridge over a ditch into a field, following the footpath sign. Turning half-left, follow the footpath up the field and over the ridge, for almost $1/2$ mile. You will see the church of St Peter and St Paul, Bilsington and the cluster of buildings at Court Lodge to your right. The obelisk you see on the hillside was erected in memory of William Richard Cosway, a local landowner and philanthropist who was killed in a coach accident in 1835.

❸ When you reach a hedge turn left. Walk to a stile, cross this and go down to a narrow culvert. Cross the culvert then climb up to the field above. Now continue along the hedge line to a gate. Go through the gate and follow the trodden path up a gently sloping field, skirting the corner of a garden to your right. Aim for a walkers' marker pole and continue to a gate.

❹ Turn left and walk along the road. Just before the Ruckinge village sign, turn left through a gate into a field. Follow the footpath sign diagonally to your right across the field, aiming just to the right of a pylon. Cross a stile and walk to the far right-hand corner of a field. Cross a stile onto Marsh Lane. Turn right and walk up the slope to Ruckinge village. At the T-junction turn right to reach the Blue Anchor.

> ### OTHER PLACES OF INTEREST
>
> At St Stephen's church, Lympne, $6^{1}/_{2}$ miles away, the tower was one of those used as a signal tower to beam the smugglers ashore. Aldington, 3 miles away, was the main centre of the Aldington gang who patronised the Walnut Tree Inn at Aldington Corner. The most famous of the smuggling centres on Romney Marsh was Lydd. Here the George Inn in the High Street saw at least one armed attack, while in the churchyard are buried several smuggler victims of notorious battles on the Marsh.

WALK 18

THE THINKER WHO CAUSED A REVOLUTION – CHARLES DARWIN AT DOWN HOUSE, DOWNE

Length: 4$^1/_2$ miles

Down House

HOW TO GET THERE: Follow the A233 north from Westerham or south from Bromley and Beckenham and follow the signs for Downe. Alternatively follow the B2158 from the A21 roundabout north of Chelsfield.

PARKING: Parking beside Down House is mainly for coaches and disabled visitors. At peak periods additional parking is signed from the village. Within the village parking is limited to roadside space.

MAPS: OS Explorer 147; OS Landranger 187 Dorking etc (GR 431617).

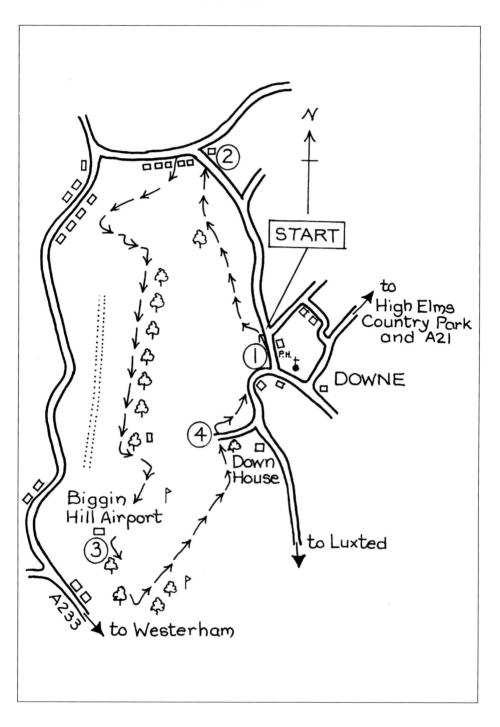

INTRODUCTION

Charles Darwin's influence upon the thinking of his own and of future generations is impossible to over-estimate and a visit to his house in the village of Downe will reward you with an absorbing hour and a half. You can combine this with a varied and interesting walk that takes you over some of the glorious countryside of the North Downs that Darwin came to know and love. For a while you walk beside Biggin Hill airfield, remembered for its part in another struggle for survival, the Battle of Britain in 1940.

HISTORY

On 14th September, 1842 Charles Darwin, his wife, Emma, and young family, moved from London to the village of Downe in Kent. Only 16 miles from town, it offered them country peace while allowing Darwin the chance of 'keeping up communications with scientific men' in London.

Between 1831 and 1836 Darwin had accompanied Captain Robert Fitzroy, the captain of *The Beagle*, on a surveying expedition to Tierra del Fuego, the southern tip of South America. On the journey he witnessed volcanic eruptions in South America, discovered fossils and, above all, researched the remarkable wild life of the Galapagos Islands. Down House was the ideal place for him to develop the 'Species theory' he had begun on his return. Here he analysed his notes from the voyage, studied barnacles he had brought back from the coast of Chile and investigated varieties of pigeons among other researches. In 1859 he published his *Origin of Species*, claiming that species evolve through natural selection and that some are better fitted for survival than others. He followed this, in 1871, with *The Descent of Man*. Though religious traditionalists of the time deplored the implications, Darwin revolutionised our way of thinking. When he died he was declared 'A glory to the country'.

THE PLACE

Down House contains thrilling displays related to Darwin's life and research. You can see his study much as he used it, with his notebooks from *The Beagle*, his microscope and his books. You can also walk round the garden where he did much of this thinking. Open from Wednesday to Sunday inclusive;

from April to September, 10 am to 6 pm; from November to January, and during March, (closed February) 10 am to 4 pm. Between mid July and beginning of September entry is by timed ticket only, so you should book at least a day in advance on 01689 859119.

THE WALK

❶ Turn right from the centre of Downe. Pass the Queen's Head and continue along the road. Cross North End Lane, then turn left to cross the main road. Beside the house, Longacre, follow the footpath signed for the Cudham circular walk. Walk between two posts then follow a well-trodden path across a field. Cross a stile into woodland, then bear right. Cross a stile and follow the waymark to Leaves Green and Cudham. Almost immediately you reach a T-junction of paths. Turn right and walk to a stile. Cross the stile then bear left, downhill, across a field, to a wooden swing gate. Go through this. Turn left and continue downhill. When you reach a field bear right to the far right-hand corner. Just after trees end on your left, cross a stile. Continue ahead, crossing two more stiles and turn left along a road.

❷ At a T-junction turn left. After 100 yards turn left across the road. Follow a path, signed to Leaves Green, to the right of hedging beside a house. Bear right into a large field and follow a diagonal path, going under power lines, towards the right-hand corner of a line of trees. When you reach a concrete farm track, turn left between three wooden posts and walk along a narrow path with trees to your right and a fence to your left. Soon you will find the boundary fence of Biggin Hill airfield running beside you on your right. Turn right, then left, and walk along a field headland with a hedge to your right. Keeping to the right of a marker post turn right and begin to walk through woodland. Continue on this path, with occasional glimpses of the airfield, for 1¹⁄₂ miles. After a slope downhill you will reach a T-junction at the bottom, with a gate leading to Biggin Hill on your right.

❸ Turn left and walk down the valley bottom. Emerge from the woods beside the golf course of the West Kent Golf Club. Go ahead along a path leading between trees, then through the longer grass of 'rough'. Walk up a steep slope into woodland. It was on the slopes just above this woodland that Darwin used to study his beloved orchids and test many of his theories. Turn left and walk along a woodland track to a narrow road. Cross the road bearing slightly to the left, then continue ahead, almost on your previous line, and walk along a woodland track on the side of the hill.

❹ Turn right at a T-junction of tracks and walk up a narrow path. Cross a path, going over two stiles. Walk to the far left-hand corner of a field along a well-trodden path. Go through a swing gate, then turn diagonally left to walk across a broad swathe of grass. In the far left-hand corner of the field take a sharp turn right, cross a stile, then walk along a narrow path leading towards the road. Go through an iron gate and turn left to return to the village of Downe.

WALK 19
A SMALL FLOTILLA BUT POWERFUL – THE DOVER PATROL MEMORIAL NEAR KINGSDOWN

Length: 5 miles

The Dover Patrol Memorial

HOW TO GET THERE: Take the A258 Dover to Deal road to Ringwould which is 3½ miles north of the A2(T) at Dover and 2 miles south of Deal. Follow the sign east at Ringwould. Or take the town and coast road from Deal centre signed to Kingsdown.

PARKING: In Kingsdown you should be able to find parking in side roads. The walk begins at the Zetland Arms. There is a small car park beside the War Memorial.

MAPS: OS Explorer 138; OS Landranger 179 Canterbury & East Kent (GR 379481; War Memorial 374452).

INTRODUCTION

Today the English Channel, and especially the Straits of Dover, form one of the busiest shipping routes in the world. In the two world wars of the 20th century these were amongst the most dangerous, with mines and submarines a threat throughout. This unforgettable walk takes you from the low-lying village of Kingsdown up to the cliff top nearly 300 feet above the English Channel. You walk gently uphill along the cliff path with the channel to your left. At the highest point is the War Memorial dedicated to the seamen of the Dover Patrol who guarded the Channel in the First World War, and again between 1939 and 1945.

HISTORY

In 1914 when the First World War began, England's naval battle squadrons were based at Harwich. Danger was expected to come from the North Sea. Belgium and France were not considered a risk and, at the start, only a small fleet was designated to patrol the English Channel. This contingent, the 6th Flotilla, was to prove itself a key component in England's defence. Ranging eastwards from the North Foreland to the Scheldt, and southwards from Beachy Head to the French coast, the Dover Patrol combed the waters to prevent enemy shipping getting through. It escorted friendly merchant ships and hospital ships, laid minefields, threw anti-submarine nets and bombarded enemy positions. Small craft of all kinds took part, including Grimsby trawlers, now armed, and two ferries from the River Mersey. The work was always dangerous, often tedious, but it was highly effective. In April 1918, when a volunteer crew sank their ship outside Zeebrugge harbour and blocked the canal, the Dover Patrol was fully recognised as an indispensable part of the war effort. Just over 20 years later, they were needed again.

THE PLACE

The War Memorial in memory of the Dover Patrol stands near Bockell Hill, above the cliffs north-east of St Margaret's Bay. It was erected by public subscription between 1919 and 1921 and unveiled by HRH the Prince of Wales on 27th July 1921.

THE WALK

❶ Turn right as you leave the Zetland Arms, then turn right again and walk along an

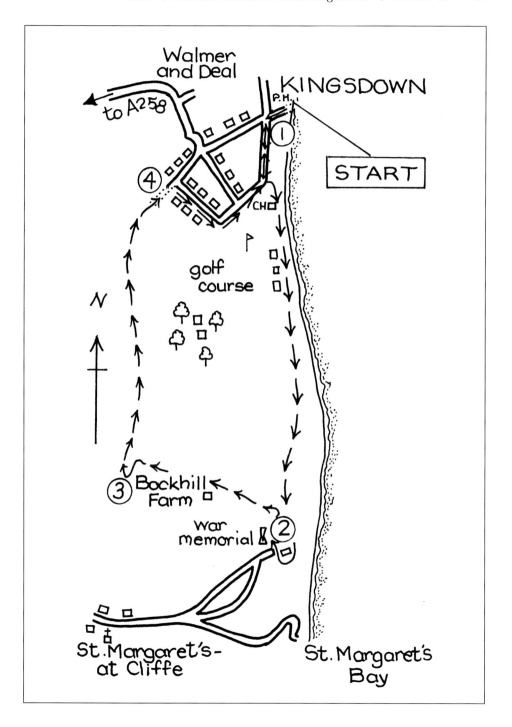

unmade road. Turn left along Undercliffe Road and walk for ¹/₂ mile to the foot of the cliffs. Ignore Oldstairs Road to your right. Climb the steps ahead and join the cliff path. Follow the path for 1 mile to the entrance to National Trust land at St Margaret's Free Down. Continue until you reach a division of grass tracks just before the old Coastguard Station, now the Bluebird Café. Take the left-hand path and walk to seaward of the building. Once past the building, turn right, then cross the metalled road to the Dover Patrol Monument.

❷ To return, turn right. Go through a gate to rejoin the National Trust property at Bockell Hill. Walk for 200 yards, then turn left. Now follow a well-trodden path between fields. Follow the track to right, then left, round woodland at Bockhill Farm. Continue uphill, over the ridge, and downhill. At a division of tracks, when you see a fence ahead, bear left. Cross a stile and walk down a slope to a broad, metalled farm track.

❸ Turn sharp right along a metalled lane. Go through a gate and follow the lane for 500 yards. Turn left into a field at a junction with a hedge and woodland. Now take a path diagonally right across the field, going slightly uphill from the valley bottom. At the far side of the field continue on the same line, now between trees. Wind your way up the hillside. Enter a field and continue, with a tall hawthorn hedge to your right, until you reach an open field. Now continue on the same line, aiming for the nearest house as you climb the slope ahead.

❹ Walk along a private, gravelled road for 100 yards. Take the second turning on your right and walk down Queensdown Road. Go ahead at small crossroads and continue along a chalk and pebble path until you reach a metalled track. Turn left and walk to the sea wall. Turn left and retrace your steps along Undercliffe Road. After ¹/₂ mile take the first turning on your right and return along South Road to the Zetland Arms.

OTHER PLACES OF INTEREST

The White Cliffs have been a strong line of defence ever since the North Sea separated France from England. Their tale through the centuries is vividly evoked at The White Cliffs Experience in Dover. Open all year round, telephone: 01304 201066. Dover Castle, run by English Heritage, tells a similar story, and has many other inter-active displays of England's defence. Telephone: 01304 205830. For each there is an entry fee, well worth paying.

WALK 20
A STATESMAN'S RETREAT – CHARTWELL

Length: 3 miles

Chartwell

HOW TO GET THERE: Westerham lies on the A25, between Sevenoaks and Godstone. To approach from the east, leave the M25 at junction 5 (south), then follow signs for the A25 and Chartwell. From the west, leave the M25 at junction 6 (south), then follow signs to A25 and Westerham.

PARKING: There is some parking behind the Grasshopper on the Green for patrons. There are two car parks in Westerham, one to the north beside the A233, the other on the eastern edge of the town. There is also parking on the B2026 at Hosey Hill.

MAPS: OS Explorer 147; OS Landranger 188 Maidstone and 187 Dorking etc (GR 448541).

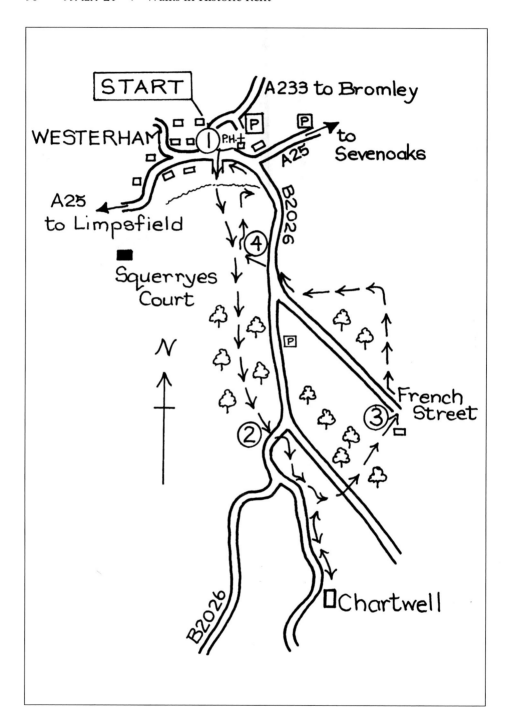

Churchill's statue in Westerham

INTRODUCTION

In 1924 Winston Churchill moved with his family to Chartwell, not far south of Westerham. From this time, the house became the statesman's main retreat and the place he most favoured for his writing and painting as well as for his other, family pursuits. Here is an opportunity to see Chartwell and enjoy some of the great walking country of the Chart, the ragstone hills of West Kent, which surround the lovely combe where Sir Winston Churchill chose to make his home.

HISTORY

Chartwell was a large, rambling house that had been unoccupied for many years, with a huge and untidy garden. From the start Churchill and his children loved the place and its situation without reserve. Churchill's wife, Clementine, had at first questioned its practicality but she suppressed her reservations and together they began to organise the work on the place. Alterations and additions to the house soon turned it into a welcoming and comfortable home.

In the year the family finally moved to Chartwell, Churchill was invited by Stanley Baldwin to join the Conservative government as Chancellor. Chartwell provided the ideal refuge from active politics and Churchill relished it to the full. From 1924 to 1940 he entertained friends there, wrote in his study or painted in his studio. In the garden he restored a lake and, notably, built a wall. Chartwell was closed for the duration of the Second World War but the family returned in 1945 and stayed there until Churchill's death in 1965.

THE PLACE

Inside Chartwell (National Trust), you can see the Churchills' rooms as they were, including the statesman's study and his own and other paintings. Outside, you may wander round the delightful gardens and enjoy the wonderful setting and view over the Weald. You can have a ticket to see the house, garden and studio, or a ticket for garden and studio only. Open 27th March to 30th June and 1st September to 31st October, daily, except Monday and Tuesday. Open Bank Holiday Monday. Telephone Infoline: 01732 867837.

THE WALK

❶ Cross The Green at Westerham, leaving the statue of Sir Winston Churchill to your left. Cross the main road. Walk up a flight of steps ahead of you and go ahead along Water Lane. Walk downhill to a small bridge. Cross and continue to a swing gate. Go through this and walk uphill following the trodden grass path. Go through a wooden swing gate, then bear left across a large field and head towards woodland. When you reach the top of the slope ignore a stile to your left and continue to the far left-hand corner of the field, going downhill steeply beside beech trees. Turn left, crossing a stile in the bottom left-hand corner of the field and walk along a broad path with thick woodland to your right. Continue on this path for ½ mile.

❷ Go through a gate and cross a road. Take the path ahead into woodland. After 100 yards turn right at cross-tracks. At a T-junction of paths turn left, then immediately right. You now go downhill through a cutting and after 300 yards reach the road at a sharp bend. To reach Chartwell walk ahead. The entrance is on the left-hand side of the road, 200 yards ahead. To continue the walk, return to this point and turn sharp right (turn left here if not visiting Chartwell) and walk uphill for 350 yards. At the top of the hill cross a metalled road and continue ahead, following the sign for the Greensand Way. Where tracks fork, bear left. When you reach a metalled lane turn right. Walk past a house 'Brackenwood'.

HOSTELRY AND THIRSTQUENCHER

Originally built to house the numerous masons who worked on the building of the nearby church of St Mary in the 13th century, the Grasshopper on the Green is an old coaching inn from where coaches set out daily to Fleet Street. Beers include Brewery Best Bitter, Courage Best Bitter and Harveys Best. You will enjoy the scrambled egg and smoked salmon, the pies and the soup of the day. These are served all day, every day but Monday. There is a restaurant upstairs. Telephone: 01959 562926.

OTHER PLACES OF INTEREST

Quebec House at Westerham was the childhood home of General Sir James Wolfe, killed by the French while winning Quebec and Canada for Britain at the Heights of Abraham in 1759. Open from end March to end October, Tuesday and Sunday, from 2 pm to 6 pm. Telephone: 01892 890651.

❸ At a T-junction, with the houses of French Street ahead of you, turn left, then walk along a small road for 175 yards. As the road swings left bear right. Cross a farm path and take a path into woodland. Walk ahead, going downhill. When you reach a T-junction of tracks, turn left and continue downhill. After 260 yards bear left into a driveway and walk up to a narrow road. Turn right and walk to the B2026. Turn right and walk for 170 yards, first along a grass verge then along a pavement. Turn left to cross the road and follow the path ahead for 400 yards.

❹ Go through a forked gateway then turn right to walk along the edge of a field, leaving the hedge to your right. Cross the left-hand of two stiles, then walk down to the far right-hand corner of the field. Turn right and continue down to a footbridge. Cross this, then continue to a stile. Cross the stile. Walk down to a small parking area, then continue along a small road, Mill Street, to reach the A25 in Westerham. Turn left up Vicarage Hill to return to The Green in Westerham.

SOME SUGGESTED READING

Bignell, Alan, *The Kent Village Book*, Countryside Books 1986, 1999

Bignell, Alan, *Kent – A Place in History*, Kent County Council 1998

Church, Richard, *Kent's Contribution*, Adams and Dart 1972

Conrad, Joseph, *The Dover Patrol*, Goulden 1922

Everitt, Alan, *The Community of Kent and the Great Rebellion*,
    Leicester University Press, 1966

Gray, Adrian, *Heroes and Villains of Kent*, Countryside Books 1989

Humphreys, Roy, *The Dover Patrol, 1914-1918*, Sutton 1998

Jessup, F. W., *A History of Kent*, Phillimore 1995

Jessup, Ronald, *South-East England*, Thames and Hudson 1970

Johnson, J. S., *Richborough and Reculver*, English Heritage 1993

Loxton, Howard, *Pilgrimage to Canterbury*, David and Charles 1978

Morris, S. and Wilson, L., *Down House, The Home of Charles Darwin*,
    English Heritage 1998

Newman John, *North East and East Kent*, Penguin 1969

Newman, John, *West Kent and The Weald*, Penguin 1969

Pile, C. C. R., *Cranbrook, A Wealden Town*, The Cranbrook and District
    Local History Society, Reprinted 1990

Saunders, A. D., *Upnor Castle*, English Heritage 1993

Vine, P. A. L., *Kent and East Sussex Waterways*, Middleton Press 1989

Waugh, Mary, *Smuggling in Kent and Sussex 1700-1840*, Countryside Books 1985

Webber, Ronald, *The Peasants' Revolt*, Terence Dalton 1980